Dr. Maya Angelou
As Seen Through the Eyes of America

Honoring a Woman Full of Life

Dr. Maya Angelou
As Seen Through the Eyes of America

Honoring a Woman Full of Life

Avaneda Dorenza Hobbs, Ed.D.

CAP PUBLISHING & LITERARY CO., LLC/PUBLISHERS/MARYLAND

Copyright © 1999 Avaneda Dorenza Hobbs

Printed in the United States of America

All rights reserved. No part of this book may be used, reproduced or transmitted in any form or by any means, electronic or mechanical, including photocopying, recording, or by any informational storage and retrieval system, whatsoever without permission, in writing, from the publisher.
For information address: CAP Publishing & Literary Co., LLC,
P.O. Box 471403; Forestville, Maryland 20747

CAP Publishing books may be purchased for educational, business, or sales promotional use. For information please write: Special Markets Department,
CAP Publishing & Literary Co., LLC,
P.O. Box 471403; Forestville, Maryland 20747

FIRST EDITION

Cover Illustration by Leon B. Howard, Jr.
Graphic Design by Kathleen Myers

ISBN 1-878898-20-5

99 00 01 02 03 _ / QB 10 9 8 7 6 5 4 3 2 1

To the wonderful citizens of
the United States of America

To Maya . . . with love

It's a love affair with Maya
    through her eyes all of us you see
        the multicolored landscape of faces
            from sea to shining sea.

America reaches and pulls us to its core
    wrapping its arms around us with its very powerful lure.

Whenever we turn within the arms of the one caressing us
    it has always been Maya's love there embracing us.

Why should we stay and get swallowed up by her love?
    Perhaps it's our need for this love; yes, to build its bountiful worth.

So how do we express our thanks and gratitude,
    for this love affair with Maya and all she's done for you and me?
        Just think of the lyrics to "My Country 'Tis of Thee."

Place your ear to the soul of America and listen . . .
    simple words are reverberating from their hearts . . . listen . . .
        they're saying . . . Maya, thanks for this engaging love affair.

Contents

Preface - Dr. H. Beecher Hicks, Jr. 9

Introduction 11

Part One - The Incomparable Dr. Maya Angelou 17
Humble Beginnings 21
Taking On Life 35
Becoming A Legend 53
Reflections On Life 67

Part Two - Dr. Maya Angelou's Lifetime Contributions 103
The Literary Genius 107
The Orator 141
The Humanitarian 155

Part Three - The Other Side of Greatness 175
The Private Side of Dr. Maya Angelou 179

Part Four - Appendix 185
Acknowledgements 187
Bibliography 188
Photo Credits 189
Index 190

Preface

THE BOOK COST $5.95 AT THE TIME. It was more than I had in my pocket. But I kept on coming back to the shelf because there was something haunting, beckoning about the title of that book. What could it be on? *I Know Why The Caged Bird Sings!* Now, in a more reflective place, I understand how important and invaluable that investment really was. For $5.95 Maya Angelou welcomed me into her life and my world — our world — has never been the same.

Her words race and leap from the pages. She writes, she speaks with an earthy eloquence and grace that carries with it both poetry and passion. She made me remember days in Arkansas.

> The sun beaming unmercifully on furrowed rows of beans and cotton.
> Crops and Sharecroppers.
> Clapboard houses with slat floors and tin roofs.
> The schools, long on students but short on books.
> The steam-belching pavement of the two-lane road that stretched for miles.
> Church. In my mind I can see her among the children at the Colored Methodist Episcopal Church "wiggling and giggling" among those who knew her but who did not experience her.

Through the written word, Maya Angelou lifted me. She has lifted all of us high enough to gain perspective on the world, with vision clear enough to see ourselves as we are and as we were meant to be. This *Phenomenal Woman* convinced us of just how phenomenal we all are.

On any given Sunday morning Maya Angelou may be on the second pew of the Metropolitan Baptist Church. She is not there as a spectator; she is fully participant. Her head nodding, her dancing feet tapping to the rhythms of the choir. Maya knows how — and when — to say "Amen!" When at worship she becomes the choir. She preaches ahead of the preacher — knowing where the preacher is headed because she's been in that chapter and verse many times before. Her mind, reflected so gloriously in her eyes, is alive with every nuance of worship, every sermonic thought, every gesture of praise. Effortlessly, Maya has spiritual impact on all who are blessed to know her or be near to her.

Maya teaches us
> not only through what she says but through what she has experienced and translated for us.

Maya liberates us
> to experience love in its ultimate dimensions, to learn to care in a confused and compassion-less world, to experience joy in every circumstance. Maya liberates us to be more fully human than we ever knew.

Maya challenges us
> to be our better selves, to stand and speak and dream in spite of our circumstances and often in scorn of the consequences.

Maya puts us in touch
> with senses and emotions we had forgotten or did not know we had. With the twist of her head, a shifting in her seat, a flash in her eye, that old meter hymn she sings or some high-pitched laughter that comes out of nowhere, Maya directs us to the place where history and hope are met.

It's a long road from Stamps, Arkansas to London, Cairo and Paris. It's a long road to the great stages, the great theatrical houses, and the great political platforms of our time, it's a long way to understand and to articulate the throb of humanity, *On The Pulse of the Morning!* Maya Angelou has shared her roads with us in countless ways but she has never failed to remember where it all began.

I do not know how the eyes of America will ultimately see Maya. I only know that Maya made me see the *Caged Bird* in myself. She made me see that true freedom is never external but always internal. She made me know that I can sing in spite of my cage. She made me know that even a caged bird is not meant simply to sing but to fly! The book cost $5.95 at the time. And I never made a better purchase. Welcome to Maya's world!

DR. H. BEECHER HICKS, JR.
Senior Pastor
Metropolitan Baptist Church

For most gulls, it is not flying that matters but eating. For this gull, though, it was not eating that mattered but flight.

RICHARD BACH

introduction

LEGENDS ARE IN A CLASS OF THEIR OWN AND ARE VISIBLE in every area of our lives. Legends hang their hats on whom they are, what they have become and their legacy. All are idolized, watched closely and emulated. We copy their lifestyles, their dress, and in many ways seek to identify ourselves with them. Their words or cliches become ours. We eat, breathe and sleep America's legends. We expect them to serve as role models, to give us direction and identity and they do. America is who its citizens, legends and role models are. Nevertheless, between the lines of pain and glory, there is a common bond between the ranks of legends and American citizens. It's called life.

Dr. Maya Angelou is a living legend. Maya Angelou, who has built an impressive reputation, is one of the greatest literary luminaries and poets of all time. Her name is synonymous with grace, power, love and success. Although many admire her, few people really know her. Angelou, who turned 72 on April 4, 2000, is one of America's works of art.

No one has touched the heart of America the way Dr. Maya Angelou has. For the last 50 years, it has been a nonstop love affair. Cherished beyond words is this precious gift we see as our loving mother, our favorite aunt, or our caring grandmother. America loves, adores and worships Dr. Maya Angelou. She can't stop giving love, and we can't stop loving her.

Though history records that many have not enjoyed her level of success, she has become America's favorite. Maya Angelou will always be number one in America's heart. We'll always put her first because she has pierced our innermost being with the real kind of love . . . Angelou shared with us her life's journey.

Perhaps, there is no better example in this world of what it means to become a legend and to prosper spiritually, naturally, and physically than to look at the life of Abraham, our spiritual patriarch. Willing to take on the task of believing God, despite obstacles and unsurmountable odds, Abraham was honored for his faith and was called "a friend of God." Thus, the Bible records that he prospered on three dimensions; spiritually, naturally and physically. Further, God named him Abraham, which meant "father of many nations."

Friendship demands total sacrifice of one's self to gain a lifetime partnership. Abraham's obedience to sacrifice his only son, Isaac, touched the heart of God. What an awesome decision for him to make to relinquish his son with only "heart" hopes of receiving a promise. Nevertheless, Abraham just grabbed the promise by the lapels and believed.

The other side of the partnership, or friendship, was an omnipotent God who could not fail on a promise. After all, he engaged Abraham and wanted him to become his friend. God and Abraham's friendship is forever etched in history and will always leave an indelible impression. Sharing his life and beliefs are written in the annals of history, so that we too can believe and receive spiritual, natural and physical prosperity.

Dr. Angelou's works exemplify her beliefs and have rewarded her on three dimensions. As a result, time has seasoned this legend spiritually, naturally and physically. Like Abraham, Dr. Angelou is considered "America's matriarch" and also called a "friend." Americans now believe, that they too, can make a difference and turn scars into stars. All Americans are eternally grateful to Dr. Angelou for giving us a never-ending legacy that has touched America at the heart of the matter. Dr. Angelou is a friend of God and America.

For the next few pages, we will share her life with you as seen through the many eyes in America. Perhaps, you will get a glimpse of the Maya Angelou you may not have known. We will, indeed, take you on an incredible journey of a life ordained and blessed by God.

The Honorable Alexis Herman

March 1, 2000

Dear Maya:

I am deeply honored to have this opportunity to honor your lifework. You are not only a griot whose words and wisdom lift us, you are a pioneer whose courage and contributions inspire us, and a visionary whose passion and purpose guide us.

Thank you for not just talking the talk, but for walking the walk — touching lives, opening doors, and making a difference wherever you go. Your life is a living testimony to your words. And for that, I wish for you what you have given to generations across this nation and the world — the very, very best.

Sincerely,

[signature]

JOHN EDWARDS
NORTH CAROLINA

United States Senate
WASHINGTON, D.C. 20510

October 27, 2000

Dr. Maya Angelou
CAP Publishing & Literary Co., LLC
12138 Central Avenue, Suite 152
Mitchellville, MD 20721

Dear Dr. Angelou:

Please allow me to congratulate you on your extraordinary accomplishments throughout your career. You are a true North Carolina treasure.

You have made lasting contributions to the fields of literature, education, and philanthropy. Your literary works are rightly considered among the classics of our generation. In addition, your contributions to Wake Forest University, both in and out of the classroom, have been a blessing to the State of North Carolina. Thank you for your tireless work, you have my best wishes in all your future endeavors.

Yours sincerely,

John Edwards

JE/ep

STATE OF NORTH CAROLINA
OFFICE OF THE GOVERNOR
RALEIGH 27603-8001

JAMES B. HUNT JR.
GOVERNOR

"For decades, Dr. Maya Angelou has been an inspiration to countless individuals across the nation. She has been – and remains – an influential writer and has affected us all with her emotional and political strength.

"She is one of the most recognized and admired writers of our time, yet she possesses a voice, image, and style that are clearly unique.

"Dr. Angelou's contributions to society – through education, the arts, religion, civil rights and philanthropy – are priceless. I congratulate her on her accomplishments and wish her only the very best in the future."

James B. Hunt Jr.
Governor of North Carolina

Part One
The Incomparable Dr. Maya Angelou

This testimony from a black sister marks the beginning of a new era in the minds and hearts and lives of all black men and women . . . Her portrait is a biblical study of life in the midst of death.

JAMES BALDWIN

. . .And all the men and women merely players: They have their exits and their entrances; And one man in his time plays many parts.

WILLIAM SHAKESPEARE

*Fleecy locks and dark complexion cannot forfeit nature's claim;
Skin may differ but affection dwells in black and white
the same. Were I so tall as to reach the pole or to grasp
the ocean at a span, I must be measured by my soul
for the mind is the standard of the man.*

AUTHOR UNKNOWN

humble beginnings

MAYA ANGELOU WAS BORN MARGUERITE JOHNSON on April 4, 1928, in St. Louis, Missouri. Bailey and Vivian Baxter Johnson were the proud parents of this "bundle of love." One other child, Bailey, Jr., was born to this union.

Bailey Johnson, Maya's father, worked as a doorkeeper and a dietitian for the Navy. Her mother, Vivian Baxter Johnson, worked for the Merchant Marine as a member of the Marine Cooks and Stewards Union. Mrs. Johnson's prior occupations were as a nurse and a real estate agent.

While an infant, the Johnson family moved to California. Three and one-half years later, Bailey and Vivian Baxter Johnson divorced. Along with her brother, Maya then moved to Stamps, Arkansas, to live with her father's mother, Annie Henderson.

It was the Great Depression and times were hard for everyone, but more so for African-Americans. Annie Henderson operated a general store that helped to financially support herself and her two grandchildren. Often, she had to leave her grandchildren alone because of her work schedule. Though Maya and her brother went places unaccompanied by an adult, they wore tags tied to their wrists to identify who they were and where they were going. On other occasions, church congregants looked after her and gave Angelou a sense of pride and being a part of a community. Religion played an important role in her family's home.

Growing up in segregated and racially oppressed Arkansas, Angelou learned what it was like to be an African-American girl in a world dominated and controlled by whites. Without cause, she had become a victim of racism and sexism.

Angelou believed that black was ugly and white was right. Hand-me-down clothes were given to her to wear from whites. Another challenge was having to endure the indignity of being turned away for treatment by a white dentist. As a child, dreams of waking to find her "nappy black hair" metamorphosed to a long, blond bob invaded her mind. Life was better, she thought, for a white girl than for an black girl. Despite these odds, Annie Henderson instilled pride in Angelou. Angelou claims that her grandmother, whom she called "Momma," had a deep, brooding love, which hung over everything she touched. "Momma's" love would later prove to be crucial and a mitigating factor for change in the upcoming years.

Raped by Mr. Freeman, her mother's boyfriend, at age seven, Maya confided in her brother about the attack after being hospitalized. Soon thereafter, Mr. Freeman was brought to trial. Angelou testified. Freeman was found guilty and later killed by Angelou's uncles. Maya thought her voice was responsible for Mr. Freeman's death and subsequently stopped talking for approximately five years. Encouraged by her grandmother and Mrs. Bertha Flowers, who introduced her to literature, she gradually emerged from this predicament.

Angelou graduated from the eighth grade from Lafayette Country Training School and at the top of her class. In 1940, however, Angelou and her brother went to live in San Francisco, California, with their mother. By this time, Vivian Baxter Johnson had since remarried, became a professional gambler and ran a rooming house.

Angelou recalls with vivid detail what life was like when she arrived in San Francisco. Below is an excerpt from an interview she had with Patricia Holt, the editor for the *San Francisco Chronicle Book Review.*

> You may know I was sent from California when I was 3 to a little village in Arkansas, and stayed there until I was 13. A lot of basic human values — kindness, fair play, generosity — were implanted deep. But when I got to San Francisco, I grew up to understand that the world was filled with people just like me. They looked different; some of them spoke different languages; they ate different foods. But they were just like me.
>
> It was very strange, because the kids in Arkansas had made fun of me — I was a mute, for one thing; for another, my eyes were sort of slanted, so they would say my daddy must have been a 'Chinaman.' I thought they meant he had been made out of china, like a cup. I did not know they meant a person from China. I had read about the country, but somehow those two things didn't connect.

> I came here with my mother, and on Polk Street, just across the street from where we lived, there was a Chinese restaurant. Because my mother traveled alot, she got an account in the restaurant, so I could go there every evening to have dinner. The family would allow me to eat with them; I was about 14 and by myself, so I sat with them and little by little began to learn some Cantonese, and to be just another kid with their kids.
>
> So I grew up in San Francisco in a global way, and I felt I really belonged. I remember longing for the fog on Saturdays and Sundays, because then I could walk the hills. It's my city still.[4]

Life in San Francisco was filled with turmoil. Eventually, Angelou ran away to be with her father and his girlfriend. Both were living in a dilapidated trailer. Finding that life with him was no better, she ended up living in a graveyard of wrecked cars, that housed homeless children. It took her a month to scrape up enough money to get back home to her mother.

After returning home to her mother, Angelou continued her education at George Washington High School. In high school, Maya received a two-year scholarship to study dance and drama at the California Labor School.

Simultaneously, Angelou became the first African-American streetcar conductor in San Francisco. The uniform attracted her and created a strong desire for her to become a streetcar conductor. Angelou still has clear memories of coming down Fillmore Street on the Number 22 streetcar. She recounts that it was a "wonderful streetcar with wooden seats."

After graduating from Mission High School in 1945, Angelou gave birth to a son and named him Guy Johnson. Seeking independence, Angelou moved out of her mother's home after Guy was born. Shortly thereafter, a Creole restaurant employed her as a cook.

Prior to being employed as a cook, Angelou wanted to become a telephone operator. However, the Women's Army Corps Service (WACS) felt that her being a student at the California Labor School was not a good match. It had been rumored that the California Labor School supported communism.

With the burden and need to support her son, Angelou took on other jobs as a nightclub waitress and for a short time, a prostitute. At the age of eighteen, Maya worked for two months, as a madam for a two-woman whorehouse in San Diego, California.

Living in a regressive society, with rules designed to hinder the fulfillment of reaching her potential as a person and a woman, Angelou managed to survive. Many social norms were defied and triumph superseded major social, economic, emotional and psychological challenges. History records and solidifies that destiny was calling her to greatness.

It's always too early to quit.

NORMAN VINCENT PEALE

Whatever you see on the screen of life was first seen in your mind. If you don't like what you see, change the reel of film, change your attitude, change your thoughts. Change your thoughts and you change your world.

WALLY "FAMOUS" AMOS

America's Firsts

Maya Angelou is the first African-American woman to have a screenplay produced into a film. The film was titled *Georgia, Georgia*.

Katherine Durham, known as the African-American pioneer of black dance

Standing Among the Few Great Choreographers, Dancers and Playwrights

Ahmad, Dorothy
    Ailey, Alvin
        Allison, Hughes
            Angelou, Maya

Bates, Clayton "Peg Leg"
    Bullins, Ed
        Cambridge, Godfrey
            Childress, Alice

Davis, Sammy Jr.
    Dunham, Katherine
        Elder, Lonnie
            Faison, George

Furman, Roger
    Gibson, P.J.
        Gilpin, Charles
            Grant, Micki

Hansberry, Lorraine
    Hellman, Lillian
        Hines, Maurice
            Hines, Gregory

Jamison, Judith
    Jones, LeRoi [Amiri Baraka]
        Kennedy, Adrienne
            King, Yolanda

Milner, Ron
    Nettleford, Rex
        Nicholas Brothers
            Oates, Connie

Rahman, Aishah
    Robinson, Bill "Bojangles"
        Shange, Ntozake
            Vereen, Ben

Walcott, Derek
    Ward, Douglas Turner
    Ward, Theodore
        Ware, Kenny L.

Wesley, Richard
    Wilson, August

Words are the most powerful drugs used by mankind.

AUTHOR UNKNOWN

I've really got to use my imagination to think of good reasons to keep on hanging on!

GLADYS KNIGHT

Intimate Moments

From the desk of
Tracy Lynn Wells

Dear Dr. Angelou:

I felt compelled to write to you to return the "spirit of life" that you have shared with me and so many others. The Bible teaches us to give honor to whom honor is due. Yes, my beloved sister, you are indeed a vessel of honor. On behalf of all Americans and myself, I share with you heartfelt expressions of love to our mentor of poetry and prose.

History has witnessed many soldiers. Each was armed with his or her own weapon and method to combat the injustices of our society. History has also taught us to applaud those who choose to make a difference. To say you have made history would be an understatement. Therefore,

Color me hues of rich, dark earth
filled with the elements created by God.
Color me full-lipped to speak the truth
for all to hear.

Color me with the stance of a lion,
strong and proud,
not to demand respect
but command respect of men
with only a whisper.

With the eyes of an eagle,
color me to see above the clouds
and fly high, high, higher,
never to touch the ground.

Reaching down only to lift you up.
Look in the mirror . . .
color me, you.

P.O. Box 244100
Atlanta, Georgia 30324

Vision and purpose are the key principles for a successful life. What we see, we write. What we write, we share. It's transferring a vision to a tangible asset and pursuing it diligently.

You, Dr. Angelou, have inspired others to pursue their visions and artistic goals. We have learned through you that our work can be taken seriously and appreciated by all. So, Dr. Angelou, thanks to you, we now realize that every day we awake and arise to appreciate new mercies and opportunities to make things happen.

What a wonderful journey you've had in this life! I know it has not always been blue skies. However, you are over the rainbow now. Peace surrounds you as you walk in God's divine light of love. The knowledge that you have gained and shared along this journey has helped to make us who we are. For that, we are so very grateful.

The Bible says that "to those to whom much is given much is required." How do we know what is asked of us in return for our precious gifts that we are allowed to possess? First, we know by observing the lives of others and the examples they have set. Second, we know by returning to others, that which we have been truly blessed to receive.

We are our brother's keepers. Thank you for keeping us informed through your words of wisdom and often controversial prose. The Bible tells us to "do unto others as you would have them to do unto you." You, Dr. Angelou, have shown the world what you would want us to do unto you. You have always shown us how to give of ourselves unselfishly for humanity. Most importantly, you have taught us to be true to one's self.

> Come inside
> Take a closer look
> You might find there's a mind
> inside this beautiful bod
> Filled with the radiant love
> and Spirit of God.
> Many have stopped for a
> moment or two and taken
> just a surface view.
> But you, my friend, took
> the time to come inside.

In closing, I must say that when I see you, through my eyes you are always standing strong and proud. Now, I see for myself what I can become because of your stand. Thank you for giving to me and all Americans the "spirit of life."

Embracing you with pure love
    straight from the heart,

Tracy Lynn Wells

America Speaks . . .

Dear Dr. Angelou:

The first in your series of autobiographies, *I Know Why The Caged Bird Sings,* has had a great impact on my life. Therefore, it has been my favorite. I also find your poetry inspiring.

You have overcome so many obstacles in your life. Perhaps it wasn't what you wanted to go through. For that matter, none us want to have bad things to happen to us. However, we all have had to endure hardships. Nevertheless, thank you for sharing your experiences and letting me know that I too can endure hardships like a "good soldier." Through all of that, you have helped me and so many others believe in the hope of overcoming.

Dr. Angelou, you have served us as a great humanitarian. Championing the causes of all mankind makes me want to reach for the impossible to make it possible. Needless to say, you have made a statement as a strong African-American woman. For that example, I am honored to write you this small token of my appreciation.

Thank you for touching my life in such a positive way. I will always be eternally grateful to someone who has given me hope, love and encouragement.

DERTHA SIMMONS

★ ★ ★ ★ ★ ★

Dear Dr. Angelou:

Just a short note to say how much I've appreciated the works you've shared with America. Your stories have given us the ultimate confidence in triumph over adversity. What a wonderful testament of endurance!

My favorite piece of literature you've written has been *I Know Why The Caged Bird Sings*. I've since made the determination not to complain, but to have pride in myself for who I am. May God continue to bless you richly for all you've done for me and America.

VIOLA MARIE HOBBS

★ ★ ★ ★ ★

Children's Defense Fund

Dear Sister Maya:

 I want to offer my congratulations to you and to the publishers of this book as they make available to readers the inspiring story of your remarkable life's journey. I join many others here in my gratitude to you for the many contributions you have made in this century and will continue to make in the new millennium.

 We honor and celebrate your commitment to creating a better, more beautiful, more loving world for children and all humanity. I thank God for all you have meant to a nation and a world whose thoughts and dreams have been lifted through your words and passion.

Love,
Marian Wright Edelman
President, The Children's Defense Fund

25 E Street NW
Washington, DC 20001
Telephone 202 628 8787
Fax 202 662 3510
E-mail
cdfinfo@childrensdefense.org
Internet
www.childrensdefense.org

> Keep away from people who try to belittle
> your ambitions. Small people always do that,
> but the really great make you feel
> that you, too, can become great.
>
> MARK TWAIN

taking on life

"YOU'RE GOING TO BE FAMOUS, BUT IT WON'T BE FOR SINGING," said Billie Holiday. Those words spoken by Billie Holiday, in 1958, have become historical time pieces and are still reverberating.

At age 24, Angelou received a scholarship to study dance with Pearl Primus in New York. Career-wise, this was a major and pivotal event. Later, in 1953, she would join the 22-country European production of *Porgy and Bess.* The production toured for nearly a year and was sponsored by the U.S. Department of State. Angelou played the role of Ruby and was a lead dancer.

In the early 50s, Angelou bluffed her way into a job as a dancer and singer. A quick study, Angelou had a winning way with audiences and these talents overcame any deficiencies in skill. Working first as a dancer, an opportunity became available for her to perform in the trendy and popular West Indian calypso style of the *Purple Onion,* a cabaret in San Francisco.

The *Purple Onion* was significant for Angelou and helped her to get performances at other nightclubs, including the *Blue Angel* in New York. Within a short period, time allowed Angelou to refine her gifts to become a successful actress and singer. More importantly, whites whom she worked with, were treating her as an equal.

Marguerite Johnson changed her name to Maya Angelou, in 1954, after a debut performance as a dancer in the *Purple Onion*. The name evolved from her brother, Bailey, Jr., calling her "my-a-sister." Thus, the name Maya and it means "Mine." Angelou is a variation of her first husband's surname.

Angelou married Tosh Angelos, a sailor of Greek descent, when she was 22. The two met, in 1952, while Angelou was working in a record shop in San Francisco, California. The marriage soon soured because of Tosh Angelos' atheistic views; she was devoutly religious. Angelou divorced him after two and one-half years of marriage.

Determined to build a stage career, Angelou moved to New York City when she was thirty and joined the Harlem Literary Guild. There, she met writer James Baldwin, author of numerous best sellers, and became involved with the political and literary scenes. Angelou also studied dance with Martha Graham, drama with Frank Silvera and Gene Frankel, and music privately. Moreover, Angelou was a dance partner of Alvin Ailey in the *Al and Rita Show*.

In 1955, Angelou taught modern dance at Hakima Theatre in Tel Aviv, Israel, and Rome's Opera House in Rome, Italy. By 1957, she appeared in the off-Broadway play called *Calypso Heatwave. Miss Calypso* was also recorded during this time for Liberty Records. As the 1960's rolled around, Angelou began to focus more on her writing.

Civil Rights leader Bayard Rustin urged her to accept an appointment as Northern Coordinator for the Southern Christian Leadership Conference, in 1960. That same year, Angelou appeared in Jean Genet's all-Black Obie award-winning show called *The Blacks*. The all-star cast included Louis Gossett, Jr., James Earl Jones and Cicely Tyson. Angelou left the show because the producer refused compensation for the music she and Ethel Ayer had written. Further, Angelou wrote and performed in *Cabaret for Freedom* with Godfrey Cambridge. Both plays were off-Broadway productions.

Angelou left a New York bail bondsman she had planned to marry, in 1960, and moved to Cairo, Egypt, with Vusumzi Make. Make was a South African dissident lawyer. Her relationship with Make became strained after becoming employed as an associate editor with the *Arab Observer*. The job gave Angelou independence and Make became threatened by her independence. Employment at the *Arab Observer*, however, helped to bring in much needed funds to support the family's financial obligations. By 1963, the marriage to Make ended. The *Arab Observer* was the only English-language news weekly in Cairo, Egypt, and the Middle East.

From 1961 to 1965, Angelou served as the feature editor of the *African Review* and a freelance writer for the *Ghanian Times* in West Africa. In Legon-Accra, Ghana, Angelou was an assistant administrator for the School of Music and Dance at the University of Ghana. The Ghanian Broadcasting Corporation also employed her for a short period.

Another occupational venue included her tenure with the University of Ghana, the Institute of African Studies. Also, Angelou was a guest lecturer at the University of California at Los Angeles and appeared in Jean Anouilh's *Medea* in Hollywood, California.

Between 1964 and 1966, Angelou appeared in *Mother Courage* at the University of Ghana. While that was going on, she penned a two-act drama called *The Least of These,* which was first produced in Los Angeles. A two-act drama called *The Clawing Within* and a two-act musical titled *Adjoa Amissah* were written by Angelou in 1966. Both were unpublished works.

Ghana was a disappointment to Angelou because she was treated as a foreigner. She left Ghana in 1966 and returned to the United States. Here, she "busyed" herself with writing poetry and songs, acting, and producing a television series called *Africanisms in American Life.* Angelou also worked as writer-producer for 20th Century Fox Television.

If I'm driven by anything now, it's by the passion of my art. I am being compelled by voices and powers within me.

DEBBIE ALLEN

I'm not an actress who can create a character. I play me.

MARY TYLER MOORE

America's Firsts

Maya Angelou is the first African-American streetcar conductor in San Francisco, California.

Mary McLeod Bethune became the first African-American to head a federal office. Bethune was appointed as Director of the Division of Negro Affairs of the National Youth Administration, World War II. Ms. Bethune also founded the National Council of Negro Women in 1936 and Bethune-Cookman College in 1923.

Standing Among the Few Great Civil Rights Activists

Abernathy, Ralph
    Abernathy, Juanita
        Angelou, Maya
            Ashby, William
Beckworth, James P.
    Biko, Steven
        Bridgewaters, Elizabeth
            Brown, H. Rap
Carmichael, Stokely
    Chavis, Benjamin
        Cleaver, Eldridge
            Davis, Angela
Evers, Medgar
    Evers, Myrlie
        Farmer, James
            Farrakhan, Louis
Garnet, Henry H.
    Gregory, Dick
        Hall, Prince
            Hardwick, Ruth
Height, Dorothy
    Hooks, Benjamin
        Jackson, George
            Jordan, Vernon
King, Coretta Scott

King, Martin Luther
    Lowry, Joseph
        Mitchell, Clarence Jr.
            Motley, Constance
Muhammad, Elijah
    Newton, Huey
        Parks, Rosa
            Pendleton, Clarence
Randolph, Asa Philip
    Robinson, Randall
        Seale, Bobby
            Shabazz, Betty
Sharpton, Al
    Taylor, E.D. Cannady
        Trotter, William Monroe
            Truth, Sojourner
Tubman, Harriet
    Tyner, Jarvis
        Walker, David
            White, Walter
Wiley, George
    Wilkins, Roy
        X, Malcolm
            Young, Whitney M.

Now, I say to you today my friends, even though we face the difficulties of today and tomorrow, I still have a dream. It is a dream deeply rooted in the American dream. I have a dream that one day this nation will rise up and live out the true meaning of its creed: we hold these truths to be self-evident, that all men are created equal.

MARTIN LUTHER KING

Usually when people are sad, they don't do anything. They just cry over their condition. But when they get angry, they bring about a change.

MALCOLM X

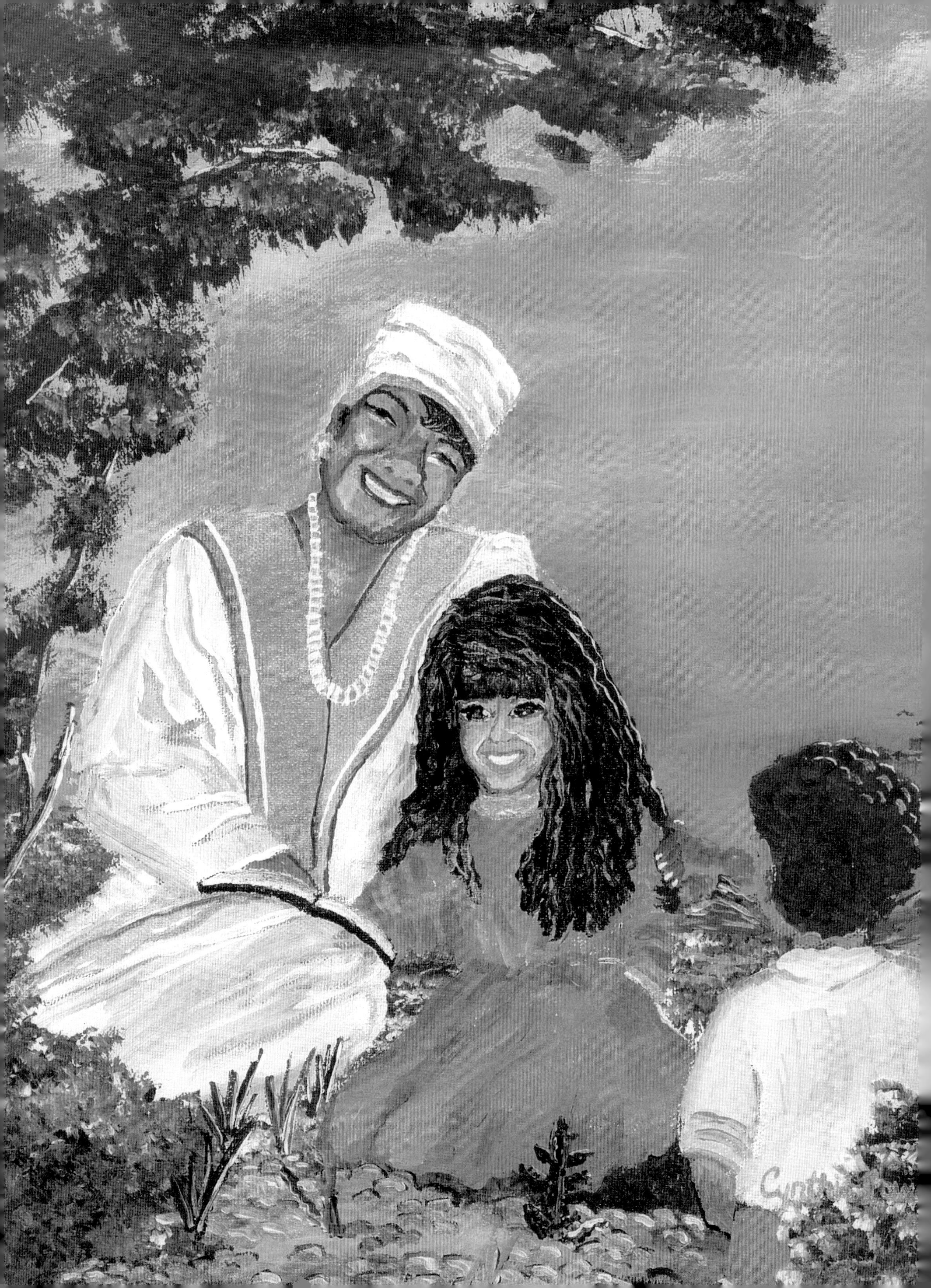

Intimate Moments

Moments of Reflection

And they said it couldn't be done! It certainly won't happen again in this lifetime. Impossible! The country's not ready for that yet. Progress has been made, but not that much progress! No African-American can have the same position that Robert Frost did only a few decades ago. Those words engulfed my mind as I wondered what really happened to make this historical event become a reality. Who or what was really in charge? Was it the fruit of the struggle, America, it's people or a higher power?

There I was standing and looking over the sea of faces before me. Americans were blanketed everywhere. A range of emotions flooded my soul. "This must represent my life's journey, my struggle, my vision and my hope," I pondered. Was Maya Angelou thinking the same thing as she eloquently recited *On the Pulse of the Morning*?

Many faces ahead of me were clear and some were not. Captured by the moment, my soul relished in ecstasy and I never wanted it to end. It was my escape. This was my chance to get away from the chains that dug deep into my soul. The marks were deep and the bruises ached on the outside. The chains gripped and wanted to dig deeper into my soul and sound its loud voice about how it enjoyed imprisoning me . . . empowering itself at my expense.

Right now, seeing and watching Dr. Maya Angelou, the world's legendary woman of poetry and prose, was for me an escape to the other side of reality. Time seemed to wander in and out to allow the essence of her words to take root in my being. Inside me, I heard her words and those voices of the spirit, my parents, and the ancestors, echoing and calling out louder than those of the chains. "Never give up hope, keep pressing on and life will reward your faithfulness," I heard them cry. It was a moment in history that I shall never forget. You see, a connection was made and the chains broke free.

As my eyes took hold of a young girl jumping up and down, trying to see over the masses like me, consciousness shook me from my escape. Turning and oblivious to everything, my mind became numb to the impossibilities. Hope welded up in my heart and it grasped hold to my vision. My mind, for once, partnered with my heart. No longer would I allow chains to imprison and bruise me. As the tears streamed down my face, a divine salve flowed and healing for my soul began to take place. In my mind, I crushed the chains from the power of the spoken word I'd heard and dusted the cobwebs off my vision. From that point, I promised to never look back. "I'm gonna make it," I said. With God's help, I will achieve my goals and give way to those, who too, seek a mustard seed of hope.

Dr. Maya Angelou is indeed "A woman for the people and by the people." We hold these truths to be self-evident that God is the giver of every good and perfect gift. His gift to America is the phenomenal woman of one Dr. Maya Angelou.

And they said it couldn't be done! Wrong answer! The answer for hope that day to all Americans was Dr. Maya Angelou. Awesome, isn't it . . . and sweet!

America Speaks . . .

Dear Dr. Angelou:

    I bring you greetings from Georgia and wanted to say how much we love you here. Well, actually Dr. Angelou, I'm extremely fond of you and your works. You have touched the lives of so many people. I think that no other poet, present or past, has contributed such beautiful poetry more than you have.

    I've read many of your books and have thoroughly enjoyed them. However, I do have my favorites which are *The Heart of a Woman* and *I Know Why the Caged Bird Sings*. You have shown me how to survive adversity and to never give up hope. I guess that's why *The Heart of a Woman* ranks first for me.

    Well, I wish you the best for continued success. Didn't want to keep you from your work, but felt it necessary to share with you my feelings. God bless you always.

MARY OLIVER

★ ★ ★ ★ ★ ★

Dear Dr. Angelou:

    What an honor and a privilege it is for me to take the time to bid you God's richest blessings. You have been such an inspiration to me over the years.

    As a pastor of a thriving church, it is so wonderful to see a courageous woman defy the odds to be a major voice in America. Thanks for not "sugar coating" your message but giving it to us in real terms. Life does not always present us a bed of roses. But, we can pluck out the thorns and make the bed dealt us be like and smell like roses.

    I want to thank you for *I Know Why the Caged Bird Sings*. It is my favorite. Keep the faith and continue to press toward the mark for the prize.

PASTOR YOLANDA GRAY

★ ★ ★ ★ ★ ★

NATIONAL ASSOCIATION FOR THE ADVANCEMENT OF COLORED PEOPLE

4805 MT. HOPE DRIVE • BALTIMORE, MD 21215-3297 • (410) 358-8900

KWEISI MFUME
President & Chief Executive Officer

JULIAN BOND
Chairman, Board of Directors

February, 2000

Greetings:

It is with great pleasure that I take this opportunity to congratulate Maya Angelou on a lifetime of accomplishment, artistry, and extraordinary living. She has touched the lives of countless people around the world, influencing us all with her wisdom, grace and indomitable spirit.

Maya is truly a Renaissance woman, who has served in a variety of distinct and significant roles in our society. She is a leading teacher, writer, scholar, advocate, philanthropist and entertainer. Rare is the person whose mission is so clear and whose purpose is so vast. I am pleased and deeply honored to have my congratulations and appreciation included in this richly-deserved tribute to a woman who truly is, "the dream and the hope of the slave." Rise, Maya, and shine!

With my very best wishes and my warmest personal regards, I am,

Sincerely,

Kweisi Mfume
President and CEO

Dr. Martin Luther King Jr.

2000 Millennium Parade & Festivities Committee, Inc.
P.O. Box 510406 • Miami, Florida 33151 • (305) 636-1924

BOARD OF DIRECTORS
Dr. Preston W. Marshall, Jr., President/Founder
Mrs. Lovella Greyson, First Vice President
Mrs. G. Ladi Jenkins, Treasurer
Ms. Angela Clare, Secretary

MLK CELEBRATION CHAIR
Commissioner Barbara M. Carey, Ed.D.
ANNIVERSARY CHAIR
Dr. Solomon Stinson
MLK HONORARY CHAIR
U.S. Congresswoman Carrie Meek

CO-CHAIRS
U.S. Senator Robert Graham
U.S. Congresswoman Ileana Ros Lehtinen
Mayor Miami-Dade County Alex Penelas
Commissioner Dorrin D. Rolle

DIRECTORS
State Representative
Beryl Burke

Rev. Mark Coats
Rev. Douglas Cook, Sr.
Tyrone Coverson
Dr. Edwin Demeritte
Patricia Ellis
Bea Hines
Dottie Johnson
Abraham Kawa
David Levin
Wilfred McKenzie
Dorothy McMath
Berverly Nixon
Dr. Milton A. Norville
Bernadette Poitier
Maxine Sears
Johnny Williams
Frederica S. Wilson
Paulette Wimberly

ADVISORY BOARD
State Representative
James Bush

Mayor
Joe Corollo
City of Miami

Commissioner
Betty Ferguson
Miami Dade County
District 1

Commissioner
Willy Gort
City of Miami
District 1

U.S. Congressman
Alcee Hastings

State Senator
Daryl Jones
Kendrick Meek

Commissioner
Dennis Moss
Miami Dade County
District 9

Commissioner
Pedro Reboredo
Miami Dade County
District 6

Commissioner
Dorrin D. Rolle
Miami Dade County
District 2

Commissioner
Arthur E. Teele, Jr.
City of Miami
District 3

State Representative
Frederica S. Wilson

AD HOC COMMITTEES
Robert Flam
Rev. Arthur Jackson

Hispanic Coordinator
Adan Jimenez

Rev. Carl Johnson
Dewey Knight III
Juanita Mond

Caribbean Coordinator
Desmond Worrell

As a musician, minister, and educator, this is a monumental and privileged opportunity to be able to blend my voice with the many voices, who applaud and offer accolades to such a well-deserving and accomplished human being as Dr. Maya Angelou. Dr. Angelou has always been a part of the black voices of triumph throughout their struggle for excellence in the black community from the Jim Crow era to the present. Dr. Maya Angelou has always been there! She has helped to remind our people and the whole world that we are all cut from the same fabric of humanity. Dr. Angelou has lent her great literary skills to the shaping of the social, political and economic consciousness of America.

For many years during the black struggle for civil rights and equality, Dr. Angelou's *I Know Why The Caged Bird Sings* was one of the most widely read books published by a black author. In most cases, it was one of the very few black literary works in the entire library system.

It would be safe to say that America, as a whole, knows Dr. Maya Angelou. I applaud and congratulate you in this tremendous endeavor to honor you.

"In all thy ways acknowledge Him and He shall direct thy paths."
Proverbs 3:6

Rev. Dr. Preston W. Marshall, Jr.

BENNETT, SCOTT & YOUNG, P.A.

Attorneys and Counselors at Law

101 North McDowell Street, Suite 106
Charlotte, North Carolina 28204
Telephone (704) 334-6330
Facsimile (704) 334-6398

Reply To:
Post Office Box 18765
Charlotte, North Carolina 28218-0765

Dwayne A. Bennett
Eric B. Scott
Anthony G. Young*

*Also Licensed in New York

When you think and converse upon the great literary figures of our time, if you do not mention the tremendously talented Dr. Maya Angelou then you would have left a hole in literary history the size of which cannot be measured. Dr. Angelou is, without question, one of the most prolific writers of our time. She has moved me with passionate works such as *Wouldn't Take Nothing for My Journey Now* and the widely acclaimed *I Know Why the Caged Bird Sings*.

Dr. Angelou is not only a writer and poet laureate, she is an inspiration. Her works evoke beauty, love, pride and strength in a people who have endured hardships and tribulations that would have devastated a weaker kind. She gave me will power in *I Shall Not Be Moved*. She reminds me of the enslaved giants upon whose shoulders we stand in the powerful *And Still I Rise*. She made me proud as the world watched her stand so eloquently and poised reading this empowering poem at the presidential inauguration of William Jefferson Clinton.

Dr. Angelou is a gift that should be celebrated and cherished. She embodies all that we strive to be. She is bold, compassionate, strong, talented and beautiful. She is an African American Princess. She is a *Phenomenal Woman*.

Dr. Angelou, Thank you

Bennett, Scott & Young, P.A.

Dwayne A. Bennett
Attorney

Charity & Company

Marilyn G. Charity
President

20 January 2000

Dear Dr. Angelou:

The most profound impact you have had on me was your statement regarding people saying negative things in your home. Dr. Angelou, you said that negative statements get in your rugs, your draperies, your upholstery and puts negative energy in your home. Now, I never have negative people in my home any more and it is a more joyous and peaceful place.

Thank you for your stand as a phenomenal woman, because you have indeed made a change in my life for the better. I wish you all of God's blessings and the fullness of the earth.

Much love,

Marilyn G. Charity

6114 Fourteenth Street, Northwest, Washington, D.C. 20011
Email: mgcharity@aol.com
cell (202) 427-7553   home (202) 726-7553   fax (202) 723-1382

America Speaks . . .

Dear Dr. Angelou:

How delighted I am to express my heart to one of my favorite role models. Dr. Angelou, you have been a role model, whose stand has demanded the respect from everyone who crossed your path. You have taught us about the love of God, and how to love ourselves and others. Love, as you have demonstrated, is the key to happiness and abundance.

I would best describe you as the "universal mother" because you have brought comfort to the hurting, and wisdom and light to the uncertain mind. Your relentless wisdom astonishes me as well as gives me hope.

Though you have been on the "roller coaster" of life, you always came up confident, strong and never fell astray from your convictions. The first in your autobiographical series, *I Know Why the Caged Bird Sings* really taught me the power that lies in all of us. Further, it showed the endless resource of strength we possess inside and how we can tap into it whenever we need. Thanks for teaching me that self-pity is a waste of energy, but giving of one's self becomes a magnet to receive wealth.

I love you Maya Angelou. Though, we have never met personally, I feel I "know you from your writings, speeches and generosity." I proudly honor you as a child of God and a woman of destiny.

ANGELA JACOBS

★ ★ ★ ★ ★ ★ ★

Dear Dr. Angelou:

Dr. Angelou, your works like *I Know Why The Caged Bird Sings* and *Singing' and Swingin' and Getting Merry Like Christmas*, are veritable feasts for the soul. Not only are your writings inspirational and find a place in the seat of one's soul, but your works are also motivational. Unless you are reading purely for entertainment and a good story, there is no way you can complete a book by you, without acquiring a desire to improve your lot in life. I honor and congratulate you for a life full of "life."

DR. CHARLES K. WILLIAMS

★ ★ ★ ★ ★ ★ ★

LADY ON THE MOUNTAIN
Dedicated to Maya Angelou

Lady on the mountain I can't help but see
All the things I hold so deep inside of me.
I too am fulfilled.

I've experienced the cost of your journey, one many will not pay.
I've felt the fears that you've faced and dealt with day-by-day.
I too am stronger.

I see the scars of scorpions you've had to endure.
Your overcoming them all has made me assure,
I too am able.

I've felt the rubbing of snakes whose motives are deceit.
And trusted in the hearts of others to make my life complete.
I too am wiser.

I've joined the battle that you fight to make the oppressed free.
I feel so elated and inspired to see so much of you in me.
I too am beautiful,
And I know that's okay to say.

I love you . . .

- Cynthia Lowery -

> You see things as they are and ask, 'Why?'
> I dream things as they never were
> and ask, 'Why not?'
>
> GEORGE BERNARD SHAW

becoming a legend

ALONG WITH BARBARA JORDAN, BARBARA WALTERS, and Coretta Scott King, Angelou is one of the most revered women in the world. Few have matched her leadership through the written or spoken word on any level, both intellectually and spiritually.

Angelou's writings have served as a bridge to join the multicolored landscapes of people in America. Writing with uncanny accuracy about the conditions that existed in America, Angelou inevitably forced America to come face-to-face with the truth about the real social, political and economic issues confronting America. The result has been an open door for many to experience diversity and opportunities in television, literature and the theater. Such courageous humanitarian efforts have earned Angelou Tony, Emmy and Grammy awards.

In 1968, Angelou wrote, produced and hosted a 10-part television series for the National Education Television. The series was called *Black! Blues! Black!* and focused on African tradition in American life.

In 1970, Angelou was appointed Writer-in-Residence at the University of Kansas and a Yale University fellow. Her first autobiographical work, in 1970, titled *I Know Why the Caged Bird Sings,* became a best seller. *I Know Why the Caged Bird Sings* was nominated for the National Book Award. The first of her five-volume autobiographical series was also made into a movie for CBS-TV in 1979. The idea for writing the book came during a dinner conversation with writer James Baldwin and his friend, Jules Feiffer. In a 1975 *Writers Digest* interview, Angelou stated:

> My friend and brother, James Baldwin, took me to Jules and Judy Feiffer's home one evening, and the four of us sat up and drank and laughed

and told stories until about 3:30 or 4:00 in the morning. And the next morning, Judy Feiffer called the man who later became my editor and said 'Do you know the poet Maya Angelou? If you can get her to write a book, you might have something.' So he asked me, and I said, 'No.' I came out to California, and he phoned, and about the third phone call he said, 'Well, I guess you're very wise not to do it, because autobiography is the most difficult art form.' So I said I would do it, and I did. It was like that. He should have told me that first.[5]

Georgia, Georgia was written in 1972 as a screenplay. That year, Maya became the first Black woman to have an original script produced. As writer/producer for 20th Century Fox TV, Angelou's film *Sister, Sister* became the company's first full-length effort. A volume of poetry titled *Just Give Me A Cool Drink of Water 'Fore I Diiie* was published a year earlier. The Pulitzer prize nominated collection includes the lyrics from her 1969 recording of *The Poetry of Maya Angelou* on GWP Records.

Angelou has worked on many musical scores for films, both her own and others. Recently, she played a role in the 1995 Universal picture *How to Make an American Quilt.* In 1998, she made her debut as a director for the movie *Down in the Delta.* Prior to this, Angelou wrote the series premiere of *Brewster Place,* a television comedy series. *Brewster Place* was produced by Oprah Winfrey, one of Angelou's closest friends.

In 1970, Angelou met Paul Du Feu. Du Feu was a writer/cartoonist and the first near-nude centerfold for Cosmopolitan Magazine. She married him three years later and divorced him in 1980. Paul Du Feu was the ex-husband of Australian feminist Germaine Greer.

Many people may be unaware that she has been a major pioneer for African-American women in the film industry. As a pioneer, Angelou has served as a television narrator, interviewer, and host of several African-American specials and theatre series.

A 1998 poll serves as a testament to Angelou's widespread impact. CyberPagers International asked a group of American citizens whom they would support for political office. Angelou was the only female named in the top ten. She finished second behind former Joint Chiefs of Staff and Persian Gulf War hero General Colin Powell.

I'm an actor. And I guess I've done so many movies I've achieved some high visibility. But a star? I guess I still think of myself as kind of a worker ant.

FOREST WHITAKER

Life is made up of small pleasures. Happiness is made up of those tiny successes. The big ones come too infrequently. And if you don't collect all these tiny successes, the big ones don't really mean anything.

NORMAN LEAR

America's Firsts

Hattie McDaniel is the first African-American to win an Oscar.

Ruby Dee is the first African-American actress in a major role at the American Shakespeare festival.

Standing Among the Few Great Actors and Actresses

Aldridge, Ira
Amos, John
Anderson, Eddie
Angelou, Maya
Bailey, Pearl
Bassett, Angela
Belafonte, Sherri
Belafonte, Harry
Benn, James Solomon
Bentley, Mary Denise
Berry, Fred "Rerun"
Berry, Halle
Beyer, Troy
Bonet, Lisa
Bridges, Todd
Brooks, Avery
Brown, Jim
Bush, Anita
Caesar, Adolph
Carroll, Diahann
Coleman, Gary
Cosby, Bill
Crothers, Benjamin S.
Dandridge, Dorothy
Davidson, Tommy

Davis, Ossie
Davis, Sammy, Jr.
Davis, Clifton
Day, Morris
Fetchit, Stepin
Fields, Kim
Fishburne, Laurence
Foxx, Redd
Freeman, Morgan
Gibbs, Marla
Givens, Robin
Glover, Danny
Goldberg, Whoopi
Gooding, Cuba Jr.
Gossett, Louis Jr.
Grier, Pamela
Guillaume, Robert
Gumbel, Bryant
Gumble, Greg
Guy, Jasmine
Hairston, Jester
Hall, Arsenio
Harewood, Dorian
Harris, Robin
Harry, Jackee

Hemphill, Shirley
Hemsley, Sherman
Hooks, Robert
Jackson, Samuel
Jones, Grace
Jones, James Earl
Kennedy, Jayne
Kitt, Eartha
Kitzmiller, John
Koto, Yaphet
LaSalle, Eric
Lewis, Emmanuel
Little, Cleavon
Lockhart, Calvin
Marshall, William
Martin, Helen
McDaniel, Hattie
McNair, Barbara
Moms Mabley
Morgan, Debbie
Murphy, Eddie
Muse, Clarence
Myers, Woodard
Ormand, Roscoe
Page, LaWanda
Pete-Robinson, Holly
Peters, Brock
Pinkett, Jada
Poitier, Sidney
Pryor, Richard

Pulliam, Keishia
Rashad, Ahmad
Rashad, Phylicia
Reed, Vivian
Robeson, Paul
Rock, Chris
Rolle, Esther
Roundtree, Richard
Russell, Nipsey
Sands, Diana
Scott, Randolph
Sharp, Saundra
Simms, Hilda
Sinbad
Smith, Toukie
Smith, Will
Thomas, Philip M.
Tyson, Cicely
Warfield, Marsha
Washington, Denzel
Wayans, Damon
Wayans, Keenan
Williams, Billy D.
Williams, Clarence III
Williamson, Fred
Wilmore, Larry
Wilson, Flip
Winfrey, Oprah
Witherspoon, John
Woodard, Alfre

Standing Among the Few Great Filmmakers and Producers

Angelou, Maya
    Dash, Julie
        Duke, George
            Foy, Bryan
                Johnson, George P.
                    Kennedy, Leon
                        Lee, Spike
                            Micheaux, Oscar
                                Peebles, Mario Van
                                    Sayles, John
                                        Singleton, John
                                            Whitaker, Forest

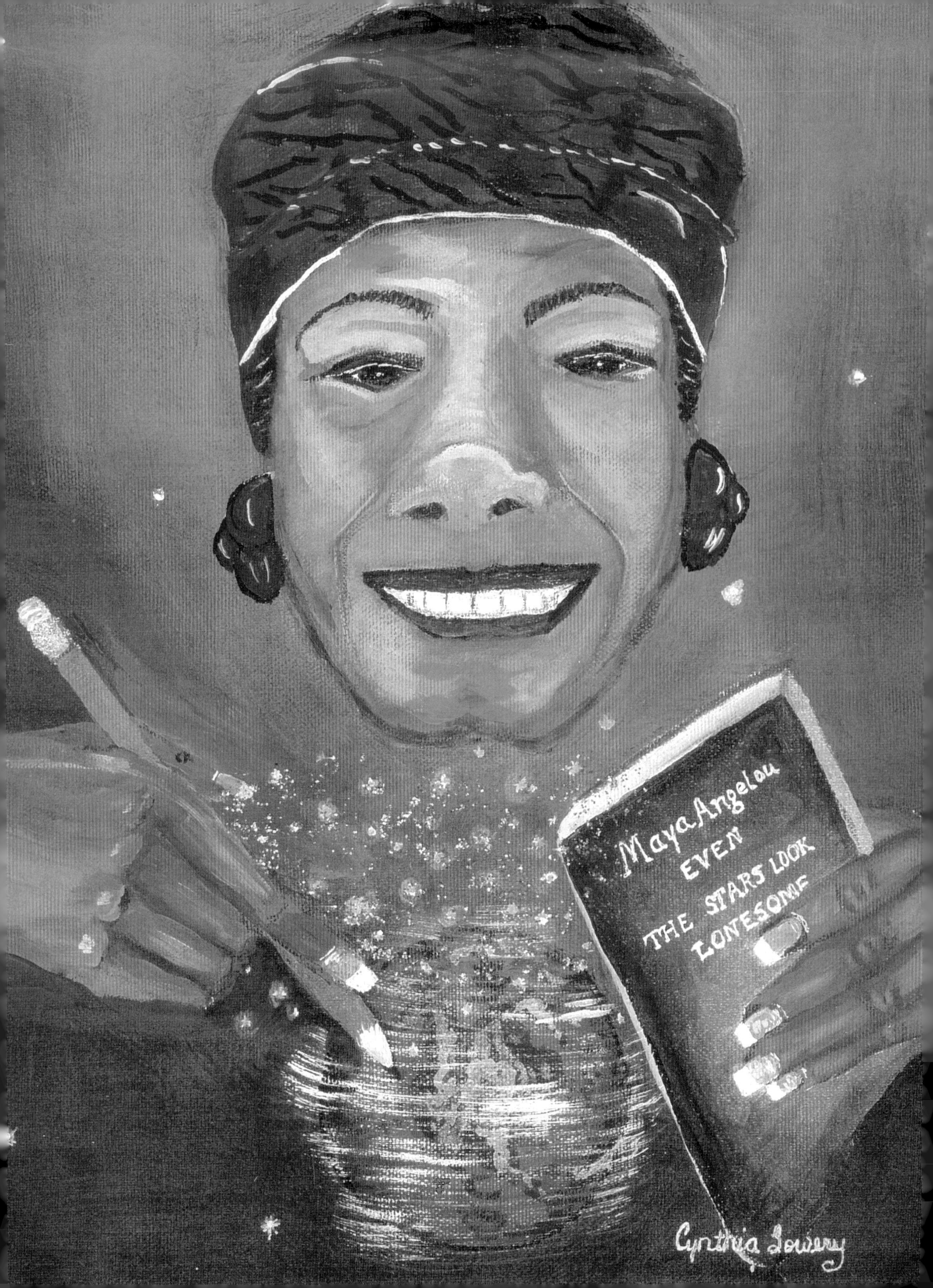
Maya Angelou
EVEN
THE STARS LOOK
LONESOME
Cynthia Lowery

Intimate Moments

Walt Disney World Co.

Dear Dr. Maya Angelou:

I wanted to take this opportunity to extend my congratulations and thanks to you on behalf of myself, my team, and more than 70,000 cast members at the Walt Disney World® Company.

You were able to join us on October 1, 1999, for the opening and dedication of our new Millennium Village at Epcot®. Your dedication speech summed up our mission in building the Millennium Village which is "A world without borders." You have said that "We are more alike, my friends, than we are unlike." Millennium Village encompasses this quotation in so many ways, that we have placed your quotation on a plaque that our guests see as they exit the pavilion. With over 45 countries represented, it truly sends a message of peace, hope and inspiration to all. You made it complete by dedicating this wonderful building that offers hope for a better world.

It is an individual of your caliber and stature that allow us to look beyond our day-to-day regiment and routine, to see the far greater concerns for society and the world. You allow us all the opportunity to look at our own individual contributions as to how we can all make a difference in our words, actions, thoughts and emotions. Your thoughts, ideas, and writings have enabled many individuals, from all walks of life, to look at their lives and to make a change for the better. You have inspired, taught, and enlightened more hearts than you may ever know.

We have been told by many sources that Mickey Mouse is one of the most recognizable icons in the world. I would agree with this. Simultaneously, I would tell you that when we think of a human being who has contributed to the fields of education, theater, religion, music, civil rights, literature and philanthropy, the name Dr. Maya Angelou clearly stands out above all others.

As we continue this journey through life, I bid you continued success in your many areas of expertise. I wish you continued success so that you may further uplift our spirits with the joy and inspiration you have given us, well into the new millennium.

Sincere Thanks,

Paul Bugge
Department Manger
Merchandise Special Events
Epcot®

America Speaks . . .

Dear Dr. Angelou:

    On behalf of the many citizens of Albany, Georgia, we greet you with love. Dr. Angelou, you have been the key to our future. Though your past was faced with adversity, you have come out triumphantly.

    The history of our ancestors has been covered up for so long. I believe that your autobiographies and poetry bring a different perspective for all the world to see. I have really appreciated seeing this in print. Thank you for sharing yourself with us. You are deeply loved and appreciated.

TASHA TIFT

★ ★ ★ ★ ★ ★

Dear Dr. Angelou:

    You are absolutely one of my favorite people in the world. *And Still I Rise* is one of my prized possessions. When asked to share my heart with you, I leaped at the opportunity to say how much you've meant to me.

    Dr. Angelou, you have been my mentor and example as a woman. Your literature has inspired me and helped me through difficult situations in my life. Your contributions and stand have been forthright and inspiring. Thanks to you, I have learned how to handle difficult situations tactfully and with pride.

    Thanks for all you've done to help me grow and mature as a person. You are deeply loved and appreciated. May you continue to be successful in all that you do. Peace, love and truth.

TUREANA ROBINSON

★ ★ ★ ★ ★ ★

ROBERT L. JOHNSON
Chairman & Chief Executive Officer

Few in the history of American literature have captured the struggle and triumph of African-Americans like Dr. Maya Angelou. Her words depict a rhythm of the African-American spirit that has transcended generations, and left an indelible mark on the intellectual and emotional landscape of our world.

I congratulate Dr. Angelou, but not just for her accomplishments in the field of education, religion, music, civil rights, philanthropy and the theatre. My heartfelt congratulations are also for her undying commitment to the inspirational uplifting of all people. Dr. Angelou's uncanny ability to touch our hearts and souls through the gift of words is truly a blessing for all human kind. I thank you for all you've shared with us.

Robert Johnson
Founder, Chairman & CEO
Black Entertainment Television

Words From Experience
By: Le'Shay Lowery (age 10)

Words from experience say to me,
that I can be what I want to be.

Words from experience inspire me,
and now I even write poetry.

Words from experience help others,
and sometimes even my brother.

Words from experience helps me with fear,
they are wise and good for my ear.

Words from experience help overcome life's falls.
now "Life Doesn't Frighten Me At All".
(My favorite poem.)

Words from experience come through someone so kind.
MAYA ANGELOU, a light to my mind.

Thank you so much,

Le'Shay

> Few things can help an individual more than to place responsibility on him, and to let him know that you trust him.
>
> BOOKER T. WASHINGTON

reflections on life

WORDS, THE MOST POWERFUL TOOL USED BY MAN, convey where the heart is and give us insights into the journey of the person speaking. The difference between today and yesterday is the wisdom and knowledge gained from one's life experiences. These ingredients, about the everyday problems that pop up in our lives, are worth recording and remembering. They are little nuggets that we should all cherish and store in our spirits, to be pulled out when needed.

In this dossier, Angelou's responses convey the perceptions, attitudes and beliefs held by so many others. They reflect common-ground experiences. Those words are called "wisdom" as they reflect the experiences from life's struggles and victories. When relayed, reflections of where one is, where one has been, and where one is going, concomitantly exemplify a person's soul and passion. That translates into a point of contact with someone, somewhere and some place in this universe. Ultimately, it touches the innermost being of another person. Thus, a connection.

In the following quotes, Angelou takes the reader on a journey through her life and shares the important lessons that she has learned. She wonderfully shows you all the important things she picked up along the way. The words are carefully chosen and packed with details that construct a clear and vivid picture in the reader's mind. With this, the readers can grasp Angelou's feelings about the joy of aging, and the events that have shaped her life.

A compilation of some of Dr. Maya Angelou's profound statements are presented categorically. These statements are called "Wisdom Nuggets for the Soul."

ACTION

A bird doesn't sing because it has an answer, it sings because it has a song.

Lift up your eyes upon this day breaking for you. Give birth to the dream.

I love to see a young girl go out and grab the world by the lapels. Life's a bitch. You've got to go out and kick ass.

You are the balms . . . you make the wounded whole.

ADVERSITY

You may trod me in the very dirt. But still, like dust, I'll rise.

You may shoot me with your words; you may cut me with your eyes; you may kill me with your hatefulness, but still, like the air, I'll rise.

AGE AND AGING

Most people just get older, and they find parking spaces, honor their credit cards, choose personal preferences in drink, have the nerve to get married and have children, and they call that growing up. That's not. That's getting older.

AGONY

There is no agony like bearing an untold story inside of you.

ANCESTRY

For Africa to me . . . is more than a glamorous fact. It is a historical truth. No man can know where he is going unless he knows exactly where he has been and exactly how he arrived at his present place.

BLACK POETS

Oh, black known and unknown poets, how often have your auctioned pains sustained us? Who will compute the lonely nights made less lonely by your songs, or by the empty pots made less tragic by your tales?

CHILDREN

Children's talent to endure stems from their ignorance of alternatives.

Young people's optimism will eventually allow them to prevail in the battle between good and evil. The optimism of young people will enable them to survive the senseless killings, drugs and other maladies of the world. These things are what keep them from reaching their full potential.

COMPASSION

If you find it in your heart to care for somebody else, you will have succeeded.

COMPLAINING

What you're supposed to do when you don't like a thing is change it. If you can't change it, change the way you think about it. Don't complain.

Whining is not only graceless, but can be dangerous. It can alert a brute that a victim is in the neighborhood.

COURAGE	One isn't necessarily born with courage, but one is born with potential. Without courage, we cannot practice any other virtue with consistency. We can't be kind, true, merciful, generous, or honest.

Courage is the most important of all the virtues . . . You can practice any virtue erratically, but nothing consistently without courage. |
CREDULITY	I believe we are still so innocent. The species are still so innocent that a person who is apt to be murdered believes that the murderer, just before he puts the final wrench on his throat, will have enough compassion to give him one sweet cup of water.
DEATH AND DYING	The only true escape is death, but even that is that undiscovered country from whose bond, you know no traveler returns.
DECEPTION	When someone shows you who they are the first time, believe them.
DIVERSITY	We can be different, value our differences, value our racial and cultural and even our differences and still be unitized in a political and a social way . . . I don't mind, and I rather like the idea of paying taxes for children to go to school in Utah or in Missis-

sippi. I like that, I am an American, so I like that. I like being an African-American and having the foods and music I like. I like that. And I like to think that some middle class white American woman in Des Moines, Iowa, is saying the very same thing.

EMPOWERING BLACK CHILDREN

Two incidents having to do with my mom liberated me to think of myself as having some power. When I was 15, and a month and a half out of school, my mother asked me what I wanted to do. I said, 'I want a job.' She said, 'All right, go get one.' I wanted to become a conductor on the streetcar in San Francisco where we were living, because I had seen women in their suits with the sharp little cap. So I went down to the streetcar offices, and the people just laughed at me. They wouldn't even give me an application. I came back home crying. My mother asked me, "Why do you think they wouldn't give you an application?" I said, "Because I'm a Negro." She asked, 'Do you want the job?' I said, 'Yes.' She said, 'Go get it! I will give you money. Every morning you get down there before the secretaries are there. Take yourself a good book. Now, when lunchtime comes, don't leave until they leave. But when they leave, you go and give yourself a good lunch. But be back before the secretaries, if you really want that job.' Three days later I was so sorry I had made that commitment but I couldn't take it back. Those people did everything but spit on me. I took

Tolstoy, I took Gorky — the heavy Russian writers — and I sat there. The secretaries would bump up against my legs as they were leaving. They stood over me. They called me every name you could imagine. But finally I got an application. Within a month I had a job. I was the first Black conductor on the streetcars of San Francisco. It cost me the earth, but I got the job.[6]

Then, I left home at 17. My son was 2 or 3 months old. My mother had a 14-room house, a housekeeper, all that. But she let me go. I had two jobs. I took no money from her, but I'd go and eat with her once a month. Once a month she would cook for me, whatever my favorite was. When I was 20, there was the biggest thing that ever happened to me besides the birth of my son. My mother and I were walking down the street from her house. We got to the bottom of the hill, and she said, "Baby, you know something? I think you're the greatest woman I've ever known." I looked at this pretty little woman, and she said, "You're very smart, and you're very kind, and those virtues don't always go together. Give me a kiss." I gave her a kiss. I crossed the street and caught the streetcar. I sat there and thought, Suppose she's right? Suppose I really am somebody? My mother is a woman who is too mean to lie. That was 50 years ago.[7]

FEAR

Fear brings out the worst thing in everybody.

GOD I find it interesting that the meanest life, the poorest existence, is attributed to God's will, but as human beings become more affluent, as their living standard and style begin to ascend the material scale, God descends the scale of responsibility at a commensurate speed.

If you want the rainbow, you have to put up with a little rain! When it looked like the sun wasn't going to shine anymore, God put a rainbow in the clouds.

GREATNESS If your intention is not great, you will not be great.

GROWING UP Growing up is so painful if you happen to be white in a white country or rich in a country where money is adored and worshipped. But still, it's very hard. Growing up is admitting that there are demons you cannot overcome. You wrestle with the, oh, yes, like the prophet (Elijah) with the angel, you know: 'I will not let you go until you tell me something.' 'But sometimes that's what causes the tired person to become an insomniac, because the demons are so thick around the head.[8]

HISTORY There have been people — your parents, your guardians, your teachers, your beloveds, your professors, people who didn't even know your name — [all] have been rainbows for you. This is the truth of it: Every graduate today has already been paid for. Whether her or his ancestors came from Ireland in the 1840s and '50s trying to escape the potato blight; or, if they came from Eastern Europe trying to escape the little and large murders, arriving at Ellis Island, having their names changed to something utterly unpronounceable; or, if they came from Malta or Greece or Crete or South America or Mexico, trying to find a place that would hold all the people, all the faces, all the Adams and Eves and their countless generations; or, if they came from Asia in the 1850s to build this country, to build the railroads, unable legally to bring their mates for eight decades; or if they came from Africa, unwillingly, bound, lying spoon fashion, back to belly in the filthy hatches of slave ships and in their own and in each other's excrement and urine, they have paid for each of you already. Without any chance of ever knowing what your faces would look like, what mad personalities you would foist upon the world, what brilliances you would give to us, what rainbows you would become, they have paid for you.

IDOLS

Too frequently, young men and women look to the mega-stars as their idols. I would encourage you to look at home for a hero or "sheroes." Don't look to people who wouldn't give a damn if you lived or died.

IGNORANCE   We allow our ignorance to prevail upon us and make us think we can survive alone, alone in patches, alone in groups, alone in races, even alone in genders.

My hope is to be an inspiration to young men and women and to teach them to risk losing their ignorance.

LANGUAGE   We need language to tell us who we are, how we feel, what we're capable of to explain the pains and glory of our existence.

LIFE AND LIVING   Since life is our most precious gift, let's make sure that our conscious life is dedicated to the liberation of the human mind and spirit, beginning with your own.

Life loves to be taken by the lapel and told: I'm with you kid. Let's go.

Let us so live that we will not regret years of useless virtue and inertia and timidity and ignorance, so that in dying each of us can say, 'All my conscious life and energies have been dedicated to the most noble cause in the world, the liberation of the human mind and spirit, beginning with my own.'

The horizon leans forward, offering you space to place new steps of change.

I try to live what I consider a 'poetic existence.' That means I take responsibility for the air I breathe and the space I take up. I try to be immediate, to be totally present for all my work.

I think we have to start to love life. Again. I didn't think about that 'til this moment, but Thomas Wolfe said in '*A Web and a Rock*' that in loving life, hate death. We have got to start loving life and the living. We have to respect that thing which we cannot create, which is life and stop taking it from people and stop taking it from things. Stop taking it. We can't make it. We can't reproduce one single person. Stop minimizing people's lives by our ignorance, at our whim, for our own personal convenience. You see, I can minimize your life. I can keep you from getting that job. I can keep you from having respect for yourself. I can keep you from being able to support your children. I can keep you from that. I can minimize your life. Yes, I can. So I can live fuller. We've got to get beyond that. And it is passed aloof stars. I mean, we are living on this mote of matter. That's exactly what it is. And we live about that long . . . to realize that the reptiles were on this little blob of spit and sand for 200 million years and here we are moths of time . . . even so in this little brief interlude, we can pinch out somebody's life. We have to force ourselves to be more intelligent. I don't mean intellectually agile either, but really intelligent.[9]

LOVE

Love is like a virus. It can happen to anybody at any time.

The honorary duty of a human being is to love.

I would encourage ourselves to love us so we don't have to hate anyone else.

I don't trust people who don't love themselves, either. There's an old African statement: Be careful when a naked person offers you a shirt.

MARRIAGE

I've married many times against my will because the man wanted that. However, two honorable people can be together with respect, love, and laughter as long as it lasts. Laughing together or reading the Sunday paper and arguing over the Newts-of-the-world can help maintain a healthy relationship.

I married a man once because of something he said. We were in England, and somebody said that women should always expect to be raped if they wore very short pants and low decolletage and acted 'fast.' So this man, whom I knew slightly, said, 'If a woman has no panties on and sits with her legs wide open, no man has the right to assault her. When a guy tells me, I couldn't resist her because she did sit in such a provocative way, all I want to know is if four of her brothers were standing there with baseball bats, would they have resisted?'

NATIONAL POLITICAL AGENDA

Courage - that's what we need. And insouciance—a wonderful word. Combine it with courage, and there's a remedy of hope. We may be heading toward new and exciting confrontations. We'll be obliged to come out of the varying closets where we've hidden ourselves for the last few decades. Those of us who submitted or surrendered our ideas and dreams and identities to the "leaders" must take back our rights, our identities, our responsibilities. Then we will have to confront. I don't only mean external confrontations. We have to confront ourselves. Do we like what we see in the mirror? And, according to our light, according to our understanding, according to our courage, we will have to say yea or nay-and rise![10]

PERSONAL POWER

Many readers will think Eleanor Holmes Norton was just born with power, like you're born with a hand. Or that I was born with it. But if you happen to have the blessing to have been born Black and the extra blessing to have been born a female and an American, then each filament of power you have, you have laid it and layered it carefully, not like someone from a family whose name makes people shiver in the marketplace — Rockefeller, DuPont, Kennedy. So I would say the power I have first comes directly from being a descendant of people whose powerful history makes me humble. I would think, if I had been born anything other than Black and other than a Black American woman, that I had done something wrong in a former life and God was making me pay for it. It is so amazing to see where we have come from: In this country, we were meant to be hewers of wood and drawers of water, world without end. Our people not only survived that, but within 20 years of being freed from the shackles of slavery, there were Black men who were vying for the highest positions in their states as attorneys general, governors, senators. This heritage is what gives me my initial power. A powerful sense of self involves humility, but never modesty. Modesty is a learned affectation that's very dangerous. But humility comes from within. It says someone went before me, and I am here to try to make a path for someone who is yet to come. Somehow good attracts good and, in turn, you do get some external power. If you start with the power inside you, you won't abuse external power when you get it. Be prayerful that your use of it will be constructive instead of destructive. Be careful and diligent and watchful that you don't abuse power to the detriment of others who have less.[11]

PHILANTHROPY   I would encourage young Black women in the corporate offices, in the hospitals, in the restaurants as waitresses, at home as homemakers, to plan one hour a week to give to somebody — to an old folks' home, to an orphanage. Just get up off your behind and go give. An hour. You'll be amazed. Strangely enough, somehow you get more back than you give. But give only with the intent of giving . . . This is pure power.[12]

POETRY   Poetry has a way of allowing you to heal yourself.

Poetry will put starch in your backbone. Take it, hold it with you, and when you need it, it will be there.

POTENTIAL   In any case, where you will be greatest, the area in which you will be the most important will be the area in which you inspire, encourage and support another human being.

RACE   We were on top again. As always, again. We survived. The depths had been icy and dark, but now a bright sun spoke to our souls. I was no longer simply a member of the proud graduating class of 1940; I was a proud member of the wonderful, beautiful Negro race.

RACISM   It was awful to be Negro and have no control over my life. It was brutal to be young and already trained to sit quietly and listen to charges brought against my color with no chance of defense. We should all be dead. I thought I should like to see us all dead, one on top of the other.

REAPING AND SOWING   The thorn from the bush one has planted, nourished and pruned pricks more deeply and draws more blood.

SELF-PITY   Self-pity in its early stage is as snug as a feather mattress. Only when it hardens does it become uncomfortable.

SHARING POWER WITH MEN   When I see a man who wants his woman to be powerless, it boggles my mind. Why wouldn't a man want a powerful woman? Who has his shoulder and his back? I think power is sexy: I don't mean just sensual, but actually sexy. So my encouragement to Black women is to see if you have the appetite for power and to acknowledge it, admit it, and then realize you already have it. Then build upon that. My encouragement to Black men is to start to delight in the power of a woman. A powerful woman is not only a great friend to have and a great presence in one's life, but I suggest that a powerful woman might be more capable of participating in lovemaking.[13]

SMILE

If you have only one smile in you, give it to the people you love. Don't be surly at home, then go out in the street and start grinning "Good morning" at total strangers.

SPIRITUALITY

Spirituality and God is linked.

The most delicious piece of knowledge for me is that I am a child of God. That is so mind-boggling, that this 'it' created everything, and I am a child of 'it.' It means I am connected to everything and everybody. That's all delicious and wonderful — until I'm forced to realize that the bigot, the brute, the batterer is also a child of 'it.' Now, he may not know it, but I'm obliged to know that he is. I have to. That is my contract.

STATE OF THE UNION

I believe there is more hope than some of the cynics would have us believe. I'm enheartened by the statements that crime is down, by the finding that some of that violence, some of the violence has abated. I'm enheartened by the fact that some economists say we're better off. All of those things enhearten me. But what I really see, and sense, more than see is the attitude and the feeling of young people on America's campuses. I travel to universities from Brown in Maine to the University of Texas and from Miami up to Puget Sound and young men and women in their thousands come to hear me. They, sometimes people pay in fact, in their thousands four or five thousand people to hear a poet. I have no rock band with me, and there are no choirs, gospel choirs, so that tells me something, they sit rapt, really rapt, as I talk about life and love and courage, and the courage to develop courage, that tells me now that there is more hope in our country than the cynics would have us believe. It may be unspoken, it may be even so, so subtlety in their hearts that even the hope, the hopers are not aware, those who wish are not aware that they're wishing for something. But as you see, more and more people go into churches, into synagogues, into mosques, they are looking for something. They can only look for it if they are hoping for it.

STRENGTH The quality of strength lined with tenderness is an unbeatable combination, as are intelligence and necessity when unblunted by formal education.

SURRENDER At fifteen life had taught me undeniably that surrender, in its place, was as honorable as resistance, especially if one had no choice.

TALENT Talent is like electricity. We don't understand electricity. We use it. You can plug into it and light up a lamp, keep a heart pump going, light a cathedral, or you can electrocute a person with it.

THINKING   Be careful of what not only you say, but what you think. Say and think good things. Step out on the good foot.

VIRTUE   Most plain girls are virtuous because of the scarcity of opportunity to be otherwise.

WOMEN   The fact that the adult American Negro female emerges a formidable character is often met with amazement, distaste and even belligerence. It is seldom accepted as an inevitable outcome of the struggle won by survivors, and deserves respect if not enthusiastic acceptance.

As far as I knew, white women were never lonely, except in books. White men adored them, Black men desired them and Black women worked for them.

In my young years I took pride in the fact that luck was called a lady. In fact, there were so few public acknowledgements of the female presence that I felt personally honored whenever nature and large ships were referred to as feminine. But as I matured, I began to resent being considered to a changeling as fickle as luck, as aloof as an ocean and as frivolous as nature.

The phrase 'A woman always has the right to change her mind' played so aptly into the negative image of the female that I made myself a victim to an unwavering decision.

Even if I made an inane and stupid choice, I stuck by it rather than 'be like a woman and change my mind.'

Being a woman is hard work. Not without joy and even ecstacy, but still relentless, unending work. Becoming an old female may require only being born with certain genitalia, inheriting long-living genes and the fortune not to be run over by an out-of-control truck, but to become and remain woman and command the existence and employment of genius.

The woman who survives intact and happy must be at once tender and tough. She must have convinced herself, or be in the unending process of convincing herself, that she, her values, and her choices are important. In a time and world where males hold sway and control, the pressure upon women to yield their rights-of-way is tremendous. And it is under those very circumstances that the woman's toughness must be in evidence.

She must resist considering herself a lesser version of her male counterpart. She is not a sculptress, poetess, Jewess, Negress, or ever (now rare) in university parlance a rectoress. If she is the thing, then for her own sense of self and for the education of the ill-informed she must resist with rectitude in being the thing and in being called the thing.

A rose by any other name may smell as sweet, but a woman called by a devaluing name will only be weakened by misnomer. She will need to prize her tenderness and be able to display it at appropriate times in order to prevent toughness from gaining total authority and to avoid becoming a mirror image of those men who value power above life, and control over love.

It is imperative that a woman keep her sense of humor intact and at the ready. She must see, even if only in secret, that she is the funniest, looniest woman in her world, which she should also see as being the most absurd world of all times. It has been said that laughter is therapeutic and amiability lengthens the lifespan.

Women should be tough, tender, laugh as much as possible, and live long lives. The struggle for equality continues unabated, and the woman warrior who is armed with wit and courage will be among the first to celebrate victory.

Phenomenal Woman was written for fat women, for those who don't like their size but will do little about it except call a friend, usually me, in the middle of the night and say, 'Girl, there's a skinny woman still trying to get out.' And then I wrote it for fat women who love their bodies, who know they are the epitome of sensuality, and when they walk down the street no one, male or female, can keep their eyes off them. And I wrote it for skinny women, those who deserve our sympathy.

WORDS

I hated the word "nigger" and never believed it to be a term of endearment, no matter who used it.

YOUNG MEN AND WOMEN

Young men and women, you need to know that someone was there before you, someone was lost before you, ignored before you . . . and yet, miraculously, someone has survived: survived with some passion, some compassion, some humor and some style.

Angelou has a list of "must read" books, she feels every child should read before he or she turns 18.

- *A Tale of Two Cities* by Charles Dickens. Angelou says, "I remember how well, even as a young person, I could understand the actions of both sides. And I loved Charles Dickens' eloquence. I loved his noble eloquence so much that I would often read the passage out loud, and tears of love for my selflessness would fill my eyes."

- *The Little Prince* by Antoine de Saint-Exupery. "This was a book that I made sure I had for my own little boy," says Angelou. "I love its beautiful simplicity, how it expresses the loneliness and the fragility of life and reminds us of the miracle of love, friendship and faithfulness."

- *Go Tell It on the Mountain* by James Baldwin. "This book did for me what a lot of people have said about my autobiography titled, '*I Know Why The Caged Bird Sings*' did for them. James Baldwin's character in *Go Tell It on the Mountain* is a spiritual young boy who is a preacher. And I thought that I, too, was spiritual, but not in the way that white people call, not with the meaning that they have in mind when they use the word. I thought that it meant that one loved God. Baldwin's was the first book I read that approved of loving God with laughter and music and dances and preachments," says Angelou.

- *The Brothers Karamzov* by Fyodor Dostoyevsky. Angelou says that "young people should read this piece of literature for its insight into the human soul." Also, she says "I think that young people will feel the way that I did when I read it. I remember how I so enjoyed being led into a community that I didn't think I would ever see. It was a real physical community — both the cities of Russia and the heart of 'Mother Russia.' I so enjoyed being invited in and being comfortable there. I fell in love with all the brothers; dreamed about sitting around a samovar with the old father. I suppose that was a part of Dostoyevsky's genius: to invite the reader into something utterly strange, and not make the reader feel like an interloper."

- *The Collected Poems* by Paul Laurence Dunbar. The title *I Know Why the Caged Birds Sings* is taken from the poem "Sympathy" by Paul Laurence Dunbar.[14]

America's Firsts

Maya Angelou is the first African-American woman to recite a poem at a Presidential inauguration.

Charlotte Forten Grimké was one of the first African-American educators hired by the government to teach ex-slaves. Ms. Grimké volunteered her services in an effort to help teach the ex-slaves who fled to safety to the Sea Islands off the coast of South Carolina.

Edward Bouchet received a doctorate in Physics from Yale University. Bouchet became the first African-American to receive a doctorate in Physics from an American university.

Standing Among the Few Great Educators

Anderson, James D.
Angelou, Maya
Baker, Houston A.
Bambara, Toni Cade
Barnstone, Willis
Benezet, Anthony
Bethune, Mary McCleod
Brown-Hawkins, Charlotte
Burroughs, Nannie Helen
Callow-Thomas, Carolyn
Carver, George Washington
Cary, Mary Ann Shad
Clark, Joe
Coles, Johnnetta
Collins, Marva
Cooper, Anna Julia
Coppin, Fannie J.
Edwards, Harry
Fletcher, Winona
Forten, Charlotte Grimke
Futrell, Mary Hatwood
Gates, Henry Louis
Gordon, Micheal
Green, Richard R.
Hale, Clara McBride
Hamilton, Charles V.
Harris, William H.
Harvard, Claude
Henderson, Vivian
Hill, Anita
Hill, Howard D.
Hine, Darlene Clark
Holland, Constance
Holland, James
Holland, Jerome
Hudson, Herman
Jeffries, Leonard
Johnson, Richard

Koontz, Elizabeth Duncan
Ladner, Joyce A.
Locke, Alain L.
Love, Ruth
Marshall, Frances Eagleson
Mays, Benjamin
McCluskey, Audrey
McHenry, Donald F.
Meredith, James
Mumford, James E.
Nelms, Charlie
O'Meara, Patrick
Perry, Richard
Pope, Christie
Porter, John W.
Rogers, Catherine
Rosa, Iris
Russell, Caramel
Russell, Joseph
Scarborough, William
Sizemore, Barbara
Steele, Shelby
Stepto, Robert Burns
Stetson, Erlene
Steward, Theophilus Gould
Taliafero, George
Taylor, Joseph
Terrell, Mary Church
Terry, LaVerta
Turner, Darwin
Verner, Brenda J.
Walker-Taylor, Yvonne
Washington, Booker T.
Whalum, Wendell Phillips
Wharton, Clifton R.
Wiggins, William H.
Wilkerson, Margaret
Williams, Melvin D.

A good head and a good heart are always a formidable combination.

NELSON MANDELLA

Character is what you know you are, not what others think you have.

MARVA COLLINS

Intimate Moments

Moments of Reflection

She gazed into the autumn sun like a queen admiring the subjects in her kingdom. Wearing a brightly colored African garment, her eyes glowed like bright stars in a midnight sky and a smile danced with the dimples on her round face. Her beautiful brown skin bore the color and smooth texture of an "Ebony Princess." Angelou symbolized an "Ebony Princess" from generations past, when African kings and queens were the envy of the world. When, too, African leaders reigned supreme in the fields of mathematics, science, commerce and literature.

For this brief moment in African-American history, on October 3, 1996, worry lines disappeared from Angelou's face. Maya Angelou looked out among the million black men who assembled that day in Washington, D.C. Those men covered every piece of land from the Washington Capitol to the Washington monument.

Angelou has been the inspiration and voice of millions of the oppressed and of black people. She has inspired generations of women and African-Americans with her writings and courage. This has inevitably enabled her to overcome the humble beginnings in St. Louis, rape and discrimination, to become a symbol of success and intestinal fortitude.

If the widely acclaimed "matriarch of African-American literature and the written word" was nervous, you couldn't tell by the expressions of this ingenious "word-smith." Angelou looked radiant and resplendent. She stood proud. Unlike the leading lady in Terry McMillan's best selling novel and movie, *How Stella Got Her Groove Back,* "Mother Maya" appeared as if she never lost her groove. She is, of course, the most respected and revered person in every corner of the literary universe.

Feisty and strong, this woman of power emerged on the dais with some of the most powerful African-American men in America. On the dais were such notables as Louis Farrakkhan, Ben Chavis, Jesse Jackson, Kweisi Mfume, Stevie Wonder and Marion Barry.

A youthful freshness covered her countenance; she glowed like the sun that sparkled brightly above in the afternoon sky. For Maya, who has often defied the odds and social norms, this was a crowning moment of achievement. It was a respect for her position, a love for her people and a commitment as a leader.

Angelou's body language showed it, even before she pronounced her support. Simultaneously, the magical words from the poem she'd penned, just for the occasion, came through vibrantly. Angelou was . . . confident.

As she spoke, her words whistled softly in the wind over the hushed voices of the crowd. When she spoke, the crowd gazed at her from afar with "boyish wide-open eyes." Birds were nestled together. Even they seemed to cast their attention toward the podium from their perches at the Reflecting Pool. The pigeons also seemed to be distracted, long enough to stop their jostling for bread crumbs.

This was a moment that would be etched in history and nobody wanted to miss it. Angelou's voice reverberated with power and truth. The world, at this moment, listened attentively to the message with open ears and compassionate hearts. After all, Dr. Maya Angelou was speaking — the living legend who is recognized worldwide as one of the greatest poets and storytellers of any era.

America Speaks . . .

Dear Dr. Angelou:

In All Ways A Woman, what a fitting title for America's woman of essence. Spiritual, loving, strong, courageous, insightful, brilliant and graceful. That's what you are to me and most Americans.

Your life reads like a story full of the main ingredients in life. Your life shows love, hurt, pain, struggle, triumph and hope. Even more, it shows how an incident in one's life can shape their destiny.

Your life is so insightful. Because of your life, I have taken inventory of myself and prepared for the future. That was inevitable and was required for me to advance to the next levels in life.

Out of all your works, two of your books have had the greatest impact. They are *I Know Why the Caged Bird Sings* and *Wouldn't Take Nothing for My Journey Now.* Of course, there are other favorites.

Can I share a secret with you? You have been my mentor. Well, now that my secret is "out of the closet" I feel relieved. It's so much better sharing what's on your heart. For me, it's divine.

I look up to you and savor the chance to hear or read your works. It's like looking into a mirror. Many times, I see you in me and in other women. Have you found that so many of us are linked, connected, somewhere and some place in this world? An awesome thought, wouldn't you say?

Mankind has never been the same since you've arrived on the scene. I certainly am thankful to God for giving you to us. America thanks you and I thank you. You're absolutely the greatest.

PAMELA COPELAND

★ ★ ★ ★ ★ ★ ★

WAKE FOREST
UNIVERSITY

Thomas K. Hearn, Jr.
President

    Americans everywhere know and admire Maya Angelou for her creative poetry and prose and for her inspirational life. We at Wake Forest University know her also as a teacher of rare distinction and as a generous friend and neighbor. We are honored that since 1982 she has been Reynolds Professor of American Studies at Wake Forest.

-Thomas K. Hearn, Jr.
President
Wake Forest University

MAYA ANGELOU ELEMENTARY SCHOOL

1850 NORTHWEST 32ND STREET
MIAMI, FLORIDA 33142
(305) 636-3480
(305) 636-3486 (FAX)
LIBIA A. GONZALEZ, PRINCIPAL
DONNA HAMILTON, ASSISTANT PRINCIPAL

ROGER C. CUEVAS, SUPERINTENDENT
DR. JAMES W. MOYE, REGION SUPERINTENDENT

"STILL I RISE"

>Content is of great importance,
>but we must not underrate the value of style.
>That is, attention must be paid to not only what is said
>but how it is said; to what we wear, as well as how we wear it.
>In fact, we should be aware of all we do and of how we do all that we do.
>
>Dr. Maya Angelou

Acclaiming the works of James Baldwin and other professional writers, as a young child, we commend you on your quest to understand and express your plights as an African-American growing up in an unequal society, with such diversity.

Your many literary works depict your liberation from a deplorable and ruthless lifestyle in Arkansas, which compelled you to identify with and exercise innate talents. The melding of these qualities evolved into a respected poet, playwright, performer, composer, author and educator, who served to enlighten Americans of all ages to the history of oppression in the South.

Today, we recognize and give tribute to you. You are a fine African-American woman who, despite trials and tribulations, used your innate gift to be the best that you can be. Today, you continue to rise and impact America's society with the spirit of life. To uphold the remembrance of your contributions, we have named our school Maya Angelou Elementary School -- a name so rightly chosen!

HOWARD UNIVERSITY

OFFICE OF THE PRESIDENT

Dear Ms. Angelou:

Congratulations on this, your most recent stellar accomplishment.

For decades you have shared with us your intellect, creativity and your wisdom. For that, and so many unique contributions, we are grateful. Most importantly, as the President of Howard University, I thank you for your willingness to open and share your spirit with our young leaders. Your sage counsel has never been off-putting; rather, you have endeared yourself to those who will lead in generations to come—simply because you willingly embrace them in word and deed.

We are blessed that your light continues to shine and that it shines ever so brightly. Godspeed!

Sincerely,

H. Patrick Swygert
President

HPS:as

2400 Sixth Street, NW • Suite 402
Washington, DC 20059

(202) 806-2500
Fax (202) 806-5934

Patricia Alami-Alfau
<u>11021 S.W. 88th Street, #L-117, Miami, Florida 33176</u>   <u>(305) 598-9300</u>

Dear Dr. Angelou,

During my first year of college at the University of South Florida, I was introduced to your writings by my freshman English teacher, an eager young woman who spoke with such enthusiasm about the book that she was assigning for our reading. As with most young "know-it-alls," I was disappointed that she had assigned a book with which I was not familiar. After putting off the assignment for as long as possible, I finally began to read *I Know Why The Caged Bird Sings* and, like countless other readers and critics, I was "hooked." Not only was the book exceptional and inspirational, I was also unable to put it down. Your book remains one of my favorites and paved the way to my reading many of your writings.

Currently, I am a pre-kindergarten school teacher and my students are now being introduced to your writings. They especially enjoy your poetry and I encourage them to interpret it through various forms of art. Dr. Angelou, I believe you are a truly remarkable person and through your writings I, like so many others, have grown and learned so much. I will continue to encourage my students through the use of your poetry and prose. Thank you so much for sharing your experiences in such a special way.

Sincerely,

Patricia Alami-Alfau
Patricia Alami-Alfau

Dr. Maya Angelou addresses the crowd at the dedication ceremony for the
Maya Angelou Elementary School in Miami, Florida

Part Two
Dr. Maya Angelou's Lifetime Contributions

. . .I trust you now. I trust you with the bird that is not in your hands because you have truly caught it. . . . How lovely it is, this thing we have done — together.

TONI MORRISON

*Hope is the thing with feathers
That perches in the soul,
And sings the tune without the words,
And never stops at all.*

EMILY DICKINSON

> When I read great literature, great drama, speeches, or sermons, I feel that the human mind has not achieved anything greater than the ability to share feelings and thoughts through language.
>
> JAMES EARL JONES

the literary genius

Adult Biographies

Maya Angelou (Black Americans of Achievement)
Maya Angelou (Black Americans of Achievement) closely parallels Angelou's autobiographical works. Though it focuses more on her youth instead of her adult life, Miles Shapiro summarizes the years since 1960. Quotes from Angelou are interwoven. Also, the author uses a wide range of photos ranging from published shots to dramatizations of her life to generic pictures. A special treat is a photo of Diahann Carroll as her mother (there is no actual photo of her mother).
Miles Shapiro, Coretta Scott King (Designer), Nathan I. Huggins (Editor). Chelsea House Pub.; 110 pages, December 1994.

Maya Angelou: Greeting the Morning (A Gateway Biography)
Maya Angelou: Greeting the Morning presents Angelou's life and accomplishments as a gifted African-American writer. The author examines Angelou's life from her childhood to her rise as a prominent writer. *Maya Angelou: Greeting the Morning* focuses on how she successfully overcame personal troubles and public obstacles.
Sarah E. King. Millbrook Press, 48 pages, March 1994.

Meet Maya Angelou

Meet Maya Angelou, written by Valerie Spain, presents numerous photos in this inspirational and easy-to-read story on the life of Maya Angelou. The biography tells of her rough childhood and her rise to prominence as a writer, poet, actress, producer, composer, dancer and political activist.

Paperback, Bullseye Books, December 1994.

Autobiographies

All God's Children Need Traveling Shoes

In *All God's Children Need Traveling Shoes*, the fifth series of her autobiographies, Angelou explores the real meaning of being an African-American in the "mother continent." In 1962, Angelou traveled to Ghana with her 17 year-old son. With a need to understand herself, she joined a community of African-Americans. Angelou discovers there that she is more American than black. Fascinating insights about herself in her early years and about African-American culture are provided.

All God's Children Need Traveling Shoes provides a vivid celebration of the sights, sounds and feelings of Africa. The essence of this series points to the hidden history of a people both African and American and their culture. Rich in language, this series details in a compelling fashion Ghana's people, and the Diaspora. Angelou strategically captures the small moments in life. Yet, she never lets you forget the social structures of race, gender, and class, that shape and sometimes limit our lives.

Copyrighted and published by Random House, 1986; Reprint edition, Random House, 1997; Paperback edition from Vintage Books, 1991.

Gather Together in My Name

In *Gather Together in My Name*, the second in the series of her autobiographies, Angelou tells of the 1940's and the struggles African-American people faced. *Gather Together in My Name* starts in the postwar years and is a story about a heroine who discovers the meaning of a good fight. At times, the pages are hilarious, heartbreaking, passionate and mellow.

A single teenage mother with an infant son, Angelou tells how she became a cook, madam, dancer and a prostitute. Thinking that she is helping the man she loves, Angelou goes to work in a house of prostitution. The poet laureate, who never loses her dignity or pride, falls in and out of love, dances, and chases after her kidnapped baby. *Gather Together in My Name* is filled with wisdom as she discusses her travel through life.

Copyrighted in 1974, Random House, New York.

I Know Why the Caged Bird Sings

I Know Why the Caged Bird Sings is the first in Angelou's series of autobiographies. Angelou describes growing up in the 1930's and 40's as Marguerite Johnson in Stamps, Arkansas, St. Louis, Missouri, and San Francisco, California. Angelou describes how she and her brother stayed with their grandmother in Arkansas because of their parents' divorce. Lovingly called "Momma," Angelou's grandmother took on the roles of mother and father figures. *I Know Why the Caged Bird Sings* is a poignant description of the reality of racism, a primary issue Maya and her brother dealt with growing up.

When Angelou moved back with her mother, she was sexually assaulted by her mother's boyfriend and stopped speaking for five years. After the incident, both Maya and her brother were returned to their grandmother. Angelou credits Mrs. Bertha Flowers, "an aristocrat of Black Stamps," with throwing her the first lifeline. Mrs. Flowers said, "Words mean more than what is set down on paper. It takes the human voice to infuse them with the shades of deeper meaning." This initiated the reawakening of her voice and music.

The brilliance of her autobiography is in Angelou's description of how she survived adolescence, overcame racial barriers and faced motherhood. Filled with wonderful phrases, Angelou writes of self-discovery, pain and joy. After Angelou recited *On the Pulse of Morning* at President William Clinton's inauguration, sales for *I Know Why the Caged Bird Sings* were up 500 percent.

First copyright in 1969. Reissue edition Random House, 1996; paperback ed. from Bantam, Doubleday Dell, 1997; Audiocassette ed. (abridged) Random House, 1996.

Singin' and Swingin' and Gettin' Merry Like Christmas

Singin' and Swingin' and Gettin' Merry Like Christmas, the third in her series of autobiographies, Angelou exquisitely provides an account of her twenties with a tale of inspiration and adventure. She describes her first marriage to a white man and the subsequent divorce, entrance into show business and how she mothers her son. Angelou recounts her entry into show business and her tour through Europe and Africa with *Porgy and Bess*.

Singin' and Swingin' and Gettin' Merry Like Christmas begins with Angelou taking a job in a record shop to support herself and her son. Angelou becomes involved with a white man, falls in love and gets married. A year later, however, the relationship sours and later ends in divorce. After her divorce, Angelou becomes a dancer in a bar. Her popularity aids in getting her a featured part as a dancer in *Porgy and Bess*. The tour through Europe and Africa is the focal point of this autobiography.

When Angelou learned that her son was resisting medical treatment, she canceled the rest of her tour with *Porgy and Bess*. Angelou shows the reader how love and devotion have the power to heal. Maya is sustained by love and devotion as she faces the numerous challenges and obstacles in life. Through this, she shares and motivates the reader to seize opportunities whenever they present themselves.

First copyright in 1976. Reprinted edition in hardcover in Random House, 1997; V. 1 Reissue edition paperback: Bantam Books, 1985.

The Heart of a Woman

Angelou's life as a dancer, her struggle to fulfill her goals as a writer and civil rights activist are uncovered in *The Heart of a Woman*, the fourth in her autobiographical series. Tales incorporated therein are about the most exciting and formative periods of her life. *The Heart of a Woman* is an honest, funny, painful, and outrageous account of her life as the singer-dancer enters the razzle-dazzle of fabulous New York City. Many opportunities are given to the reader to cheer and think about their own life experiences.

Angelou tells us how her passion for writing blazes anew at the Harlem Writers Guild. She shares her debut at the Apollo Theatre and her meeting with Malcolm X. She further chronicles the joys of motherhood and watches her beloved and cherished son become a man.

Political activism was a significant segment in Angelou's life. Angelou tells how she organized a theatrical benefit for the Reverend Dr. Martin Luther King, Jr. Afterwards, she became the director of the New York Southern Christian Leadership Conference. Her civil rights involvement would soon bring her into the company of several African freedom fighters such as Oliver Tamob and Vusumzi Make. She later marries Make and follows him to Africa.

The Heart of a Woman is filled with unforgettable vignettes of new things with African-American celebrities whom Maya adopts as mentors. Jazz musicians Max Roach and Abbey Lincoln, actors Godfrey Cambridge and James Earl Jones, writers John Ellins and Paul Marshall, and singer Billie Holliday are named.

Published by Random House in 1981; Paperback edition Bantam Books, 1997; Audiocassette edition, Random House, 1997; Large print edition, Boston: Compass Press, 1997.

Co-Authored Works

Bearing Witness: Contemporary Works by African-American Women Artists

Bearing Witness: Contemporary Works by African-American Women Artists accompanies an exhibition of the work of 25 African-American women artists, including Carrie Mae Weems, Lorna Simpson and Faith Ringgold. There are essays, paintings, prints and sculptures.

International Publications, 1996; paperback ed. Rizzoli, 1996.

Maya Angelou writes like a song, and like the truth.

NEW YORK TIMES BOOK REVIEW

Everything about Maya Angelou is transcendental. She has something to tell you now. Listen.

THE WASHINGTON POST BOOK WORLD

If you don't know [Maya Angelou] yet, now is as good a time as any to jump in and partake of her bounteous wisdom.

LOS ANGELES TIMES

Angelou's voice is spellbinding, bubbling with rhythm, vivid with lessons.

THE MIAMI HERALD

Angelou is a force of nature.

CHICAGO SUN-TIMES

A sort of wit and wisdom of Angelou, culled from a lifetime of adversity and overcoming.

THE DENVER POST

How to Make an American Quilt

How to Make an American Quilt explores women of the past and today as they come together for a unique female experience. As the women gather year after year to share their stories, their lives and experiences, they build a pattern that each female can identify with. Likewise, each can find comfort and a type of warmth drawn from related experiences. Angelou also appears in the motion picture that premiered in 1995.

Paperback, Ballantine in May 1994.

Contributions to Published Works

My Soul's Been Anchored

My Soul's Been Anchored is a preacher's heritage of faith, calling us to make a difference in the world today. This book is authored by Dr. H. Beecher Hicks, Jr., with the foreword written by Dr. Maya Angelou.

Hardcover, 1998. ZondervanPublishingHouse. Grand Rapids, Michigan.

Not Without Laughter

Maya Angelou writes the "new" introduction to this classic of African-American literature. *Not Without Laughter* presents a novel filled with lyricism and humor. The setting, in a small Kansas town in the early twentieth century, shows Langston Hughes' influence as a force in African-American literature. *Not Without Laughter* reflects the joys and hardships of a African-American boy growing into manhood.

Langston Hughes with the introduction by Maya Angelou. Scribner, 299 pages, 1995.

The Negritude Poets: An Anthology of Translations from the French

The Negritude Poets: An Anthology of Translations from the French is an incredible collection of some of the world's most powerful and gifted poets. Angelou brilliantly designs this classic.

Ellen C. Kennedy and Maya Angelou. Paperback, 284 pages; Thunder's Mouth Press, 1989.

Trials, Tribulations, and Celebrations: African-American Perspectives on Health, Illness, Aging, and Loss

African-American perspectives and insights are presented on the various phases of an African-American's life cycle. Celebrated writers such as Alice Walker, Langston Hughes, Gwendolyn Brooks, James Weldon Johnson, and Maya Angelou, provide poignant and powerful discussions on this topic. Areas discussed include faith, mortality, motherhood, friendship, and customs and prejudices effecting the African-American community.

Marian Gray (Editor) with the literary collaboration of Dr. Lois LaCivita Nixon. Paperback, 352 pages; Intercultural Press, 1991.

Man's greatness consists in his ability to do and the proper application of his powers to things needed to be done.

FREDERICK DOUGLAS

Grab the broom of anger and drive off the beast of fear.

ZORA NEALE HURSTON

No woman can be handsome by the force of features alone, any more that she can be witty by only the help of speech.

LANGSTON HUGHES

It's not the load that breaks you down, it's the way you carry it.

LENA HORNE

Conversations With Maya Angelou

Black Pearls: The Poetry of Maya Angelou

In *Black Pearls: The Poetry of Maya Angelou*, Angelou reads her poetry, talks about a three-year period in her childhood where she refused to speak, and discusses *I Know Why The Caged Bird Sings*. Angelou explains her most prized accomplishment as a writer. She further discusses her views about being beautiful, musical, sexy, sassy and black.

Audio CD; Rhino Records, 1998.

Maya Angelou: Making Magic in the World

Maya Angelou weaves a tapestry of her life's journey. Listeners travel with Dr. Angelou from the deep South to the heart of Africa and back again. She shares with listeners the memories of those mentors and teachers who profoundly influenced her life.

Audiocassette ed. by Hay House Audio, 1998.

Cooking

Caribbean and African Cooking

Caribbean and African Cooking offers delicious Caribbean and African recipes as written by Rosamund Grant and Maya Angelou.

Rosamund Grant and Maya Angelou: Interlink Pub Group, 1997.

Essays

Even the Stars Look Lonesome

The 20 brief, anecdotal, and spicily provocative essays in *Even the Stars Look Lonesome* are filled with Angelou's experiences and feelings. *Even the Stars Look Lonesome* is a "quick read" book that covers a wide variety of topics. Each chapter is an essay, a separate story and rather poetic. Each is insightful and entertaining. A collection of her personal experiences and writings, Angelou shares what she deeply cares about. *Even the Stars Look Lonesome* contains many of her favorite stories and examines the mixed blessings of success. The sister volume to the 1993 collection called *Wouldn't Take Nothing for My Journey Now, Even the Stars Look Lonesome* is rich with detail and passion.

Angelou describes how she supported her son as a nightclub singer during the 1950's. Also, she tells how she has mastered the skill of accepting the rewards and demands of fame with grace. Further, she gives candid and vividly crafted homilies about how she makes good use of her visibility. Angelou tells her thoughts on marriage, motherhood, African creativity and its influence on African-American history and the value of art and solitude.

Even the Stars Look Lonesome is rather poetic as well as entertaining and educational, and was nominated for the 1998 Grammy for best spoken word for a non-musical album.

Random House, 1997. 128p.; paperback large print ed. Thorndike, 1997.

Wouldn't Take Nothing for My Journey Now

Wouldn't Take Nothing for My Journey Now presents spiritual autobiographical essays that warm and sear the heart. In one essay, Angelou attempts to get a group of African-American professional men to accept her for who she is. Ironically, she later realizes that she did not do the same for the men in her life.

Hardcover, Random House, 1993. 141 p.; Paperback Bantam Doubleday Dell, 1997.

Fiction

Mrs. Flowers: A Moment of Friendship

Marguerite Johnson, better known as Maya Angelou, was raised by her grandmother in Stamps, Arkansas. After being sexually assaulted by her mother's boyfriend, Angelou did not speak for five years. Mrs. Flowers, an African-American aristocrat in Stamps, "threw Maya her first lifeline." Because of her friendship with Mrs. Flowers, Maya developed an appreciation for literature and raised her self-esteem. *Mrs. Flowers: A Moment of Friendship* was illustrated by Etienne Delessert.

Redpath Press, 1986; Minneapolis, MN.

Juvenile Biographies

Greeting the Morning

Greeting the Morning examines Angelou's life from childhood to her rise as a prominent writer.

Written by Sarah E. King and Maya Angelou. Brookfield, Conn.; Millbrook Press, 1994. Ages 4-8.

I Have a Dream: Maya Angelou; Woman of Words, Deeds and Dreams

Dr. Maya Angelou's life is described and written for young readers.

Kallen, Stuart A. Edina, Minn.: Abdo & Daughters, 1993; Distributed by Rockbottom Books. Ages 9-12.

Journey of the Heart

Author Jayne Pettit writes an account of childhood trauma that is overcome with the help of one's family and the community. *Journey of the Heart* is a middle-grade reader biography based on Angelou's first autobiographical work.

New York: Lodestar, 1996. Ages 9-12.

Maya Angelou

Miles Shapiro and Maya Angelou begin this juvenile biography with an introductory essay by Coretta Scott King. *Maya Angelou* is a description of and discusses the life and work of the famous author.

New York: Chelsea House, 1994. Ages 9-12.

Maya Angelou by Nancy Shuker

Nancy Shuker focuses on Angelou's struggles as a woman, mother and an artist. She portrays Angelou's life as a poet, musician and actress.

Englewood Cliffs, NJ. Silver Burdett, 1990.

Meet Maya Angelou

Meet Maya Angelou is a classic juvenile biography. Written by Valerie Spain, *Meet Maya Angelou* describes Angelou's life from a rough childhood to her rise to prominence as a poet, writer, actress and dancer.

New York: Random House, 1994. Ages 9-12.

Maya Angelou: More than a Poet

The life of Maya Angelou as an author, poet and educator is portrayed in *Maya Angelou: More than a Poet*. Elaine Lisandrelli and Angelou authored this biography.

Springfield, NJ; Enslow Publishers, 1996.

Movies/Feature Films

Down in the Delta

Down in the Delta is about an African-American family torn between its roots in the South and the Chicago projects. Angelou makes her directorial debut with this movie. *Down in the Delta* co-stars Alfre Woodard and Wesley Snipes.

Georgia, Georgia

In 1972, Angelou wrote the original screenplay and musical score for *Georgia, Georgia*. The film is about an African-American singer who involves herself with a white singer and American defectors.

Georgia, Georgia is the first original script written and produced by a African-American woman. The film was directed by Stig Bjorkman and starred Diana Sands, Dirk Benedict and Minnie Gentry.

How to Make an American Quilt

How to Make an American Quilt explores the lives of three generations of women in the small town of Grasse, California. There, three generations of women and their lives are explored. Using a quilt as a backdrop, each woman's story represents a square on the quilt. *How to Make an American Quilt*, which premiered in 1995, describes how these women, with different experiences, come together for a unique female experience. As the women gather year after year to share their stories, their lives and experiences, they build a pattern that each woman can identify with. Likewise, each can find comfort and a type of warmth drawn from common experiences.

Angelou plays the role of "Anna," the master quilter. Anna first comes to the sisters as an unwed and pregnant woman. She stays on as a housekeeper and becomes friends with the other women. Other personalities featured in this film include Anne Bancroft, Alfre Woodard, Winona Ryder, Ellen Burstyn, Kata Nelligan, Jean Simmons and Lois Smith.

Poetic Justice

John Singleton produced *Poetic Justice* in 1993, which featured poetry by Maya Angelou. Angelou also appeared briefly in the role of "Aunt June." The foreword to this work was written by filmmaker Spike Lee.

Picture Books

Kofi and His Magic

Kofi, a seven-year-old West African boy, narrates this story about his imaginary magical trips to other places in Ghana. He uses magic, by closing and opening his eyes, to leave his hometown to a journey, then to a place up north. The strikingly colorful and vibrant photos show the various places within West Africa. Photos convey positive and realistic portraits of powerful men and women wearing traditional African cloth.

By Maya Angelou and Margaret Courtney-Clarke. With photos by Margaret Courtney-Clarke. Hardcover ed. Clarkson Potter Publications, 1996. 44p. Ages 4-8 Picture Book.

Life Doesn't Frighten Me

Dramatic pictures illustrate Angelou's poem, *Life Doesn't Frighten Me*, which confronts our archetypal fears.

By Maya Angelou, Sara Boyers and Jean Michel Basquiat, illustrator. Hardcover ed. Stewart Tabori & Chang, 1993. Ages 4-8.

My Painted House, My Friendly Chicken and Me

Thandi, an 8-year old Ndebele girl from a South African village, her family, and her pet chicken are the main focus of this picture book. *My Painted House, My Friendly Chicken and Me* is delightful and humorous. Mural art by the Ndebele women of Africa are showcased, while introducing young readers to African culture. Namibian-born photojournalist Margaret Courtney-Clarke, uses over 70 expertly composed color photographs to record the passing of traditions from parent to child. Angelou's narrative and Clarke's ravishing photos are perfect.

By Maya Angelou and Margaret Courtney-Clarke. Photos by Margaret Courtney-Clarke. Hardcover Crown Pub., 1994, paperback ed. Clarkson Potter, 1996. Ages 4-8.

Soul Looks Back in Wonder

Poems by Angelou, Langston Hughes, and Askia Toure are illustrated with Tom Feelings' artwork in *Soul Looks Back in Wonder*. Dramatic combinations of collages, sweeping backgrounds, and picturesque landscapes are used to celebrate African creativity. Feelings uses pictures he sketched on travel throughout Senegal, Ghana, Guyana and the United States. In *Soul Looks Back in Wonder*, Tom Feelings provides the artwork for poems that portray the strength and character of adults and children.

New York: Dial Books, 1993. Illustrated by Tom Feelings.

Poetry

A Brave and Startling Truth

A Brave and Startling Truth is the famous and memorable poem first read by Angelou at the 50th anniversary of the founding of the United Nations. Moving and full of wisdom, Angelou's poem is a message of hope for mankind and will unequivocally inspire readers.

Copyright 1995, Random House.

And Still I Rise

And Still I Rise is a distinctive collection of poetry full of uplifting rhythms of remembering and love. The collection includes such poems as: "Ain't That Bad;" "Bump D'bump;" "Mrs. V.B.;" "Life Doesn't Frighten Me;" "Phenomenal Woman;" "Still I Rise;" "Thank You, Lord;" and, "Woman Work."

Copyright 1978, Random House; Audiocassette Random House, 1996.

Just Give Me a Cool Drink of Water 'Fore I Diiie

A two-part anthology, *Just Give Me a Cool Drink of Water 'Fore I Diiie*, is Angelou's first

Success is the sweetest revenge.

VANESSA WILLIAMS

Words are energy. Use them to encourage and inspire. Check the bad, but encourage the good.

STEVIE WONDER

It's the moment you think you can't that you realize you can.

CELINE DION

If you really want something you can figure out how to make it happen.

CHER

If I could come back as anything — I'd be a bird, first, but definitely the command key is my second choice.

NIKKI GIOVANNI

I say that democracy can never prove itself beyond cavil, until it founds and luxuriantly grows its own forms of art, poems, schools, theology, displacing all that exists, or that has been produced anywhere in the past, under opposite influences.

WALT WHITMAN

poetry collection. The anthology reflects on love, memory and nostalgia, as well as a racist society and the inherent confrontations.

Hardcover edition, Random House, 1971 and 1997. Audiocassette ed. Random House, 1997.

I Shall Not Be Moved

A classic and vintage Maya Angelou is presented in this three volume set. Included is her first poetry collection titled *Just Give Me a Cool Drink of Water 'Fore I Diiie*. Other favorite poems in this collection of treasured works are: "Equality;" "Fightin' Was Natural;" "Forgive;" "Known To Eve And Me;" "Our Grandmothers;" "Preacher, Don't Send Me;" "Savior;" "These Yet To Be United States;" and "Worker's Song."

Rep. edition paperback: Bantam Books, 1991; Hardcover ed. Random House, 1990; Audiocassette ed. Random House, 1997.

Maya Angelou: Poems: Just Give Me a Cool Drink of Water 'Fore I Diiie

The discovery and celebration of life is detailed with heartfelt expressions as only Angelou can. *Maya Angelou: Poems: Just Give Me a Cool Drink of Water 'Fore I Diiie* is a deeply reflective and moving volume of poetry.

Reprint edition, Bantam, 1986.

Now Sheba Sings the Song

In *Now Sheba Sings the Song*, Caldecott Award-winning illustrator Tom Feelings teamed up with Angelou to combine verse and sepia-toned illustrations as a "beautiful song to black women."

Dutton/Dial, 1987. Paperback: Plume, 1994.

Oh Pray My Wings Are Gonna Fit Me Well

Oh Pray My Wings Are Gonna Fit Me Well is a collection of 36 poems that remembers the past of African-Americans. Though their past consists of loneliness, losses and destruction, Angelou's multi-faceted voice is powerfully reflected in this collection of poetry.

Hardcover edition, Random House, 1975. Audiocassette ed. Random House, 1997.

On the Pulse of Morning; the Inaugural Poem

The nation was captivated by Angelou's *On the Pulse of Morning*, at the inauguration of President William Jefferson Clinton. It quickly became a national bestseller. The inaugural poem won the 1994 Grammy award for best spoken word for a non-musical album.

Hardcover, Random House, 1993; Paperback Random House, 1993.

Phenomenal Woman; Four Poems Celebrating Women
Phenomenal Women, And Still I Rise, Weekend Glory, and *Our Grandmothers,* are among the most acclaimed of Maya Angelou's poems. Women are honored and presented reverently, vividly, openly and enthusiastically. This collection is dedicated to Vivian Baxter, Angelou's mother, whom she called "phenomenal." Angelou received the 1996 Grammy award for best spoken word for non-musical album for the poem *Phenomenal Woman.*
Hardcover edition Random House, 1993; Audiocassette ed. Random House, 1995.

Poetic Justice
Poetic Justice was written by John Singleton in 1993. Angelou, who appeared briefly in the role of "Aunt June," also wrote poetry for the film. The foreword to this work was written by filmmaker Spike Lee.

Shaker, Why Don't You Sing?
Shaker, Why Don't You Sing? is a wonderful collection of lyrical and dramatic poetry. The poems focus on parting, longing, freedom, shattered dreams and love. Other poems speak of Saturday-night partying and the smells and sounds of southern cities.
First edition in hardcover, Random House, 1983.

The Beacon Book of Essays by Contemporary American Women
The Beacon Book of Essays by Contemporary American Women is a collection of several essays written by well-known authors on a wide variety of topics facing women. Areas addressed by these women writers include children, families, infertility, rape, lovers, and the complexities of ethnic identity. Classics by Maya Angelou and Joan Didion are featured, along with writings by Gwendolyn Brooks, Annie Dillard, Margaret Mead and others.
Edited by Wendy Martin; Literature/Women's Studies; Hardcover; Beacon Publishing; Fall 1995.

The Black Family Pledge
The Black Family Pledge was written by Dr. Angelou to commemorate the solidarity of African-American family members at Kawanzaa. During the main feast, called the Karamu, different family members take turns at reciting a stanza of the pledge. At the end, the pledge is read in unison by participating family members. *The Black Family Pledge* was read at the Black Family Reunion on the National Mall in Washington, D.C. The event was sponsored by the National Council of Negro Women and the National Park Service.
Copyright 1997, Dr. Maya Angelou.

The Complete Collected Poems of Maya Angelou

The Complete Collected Poems of Maya Angelou covers everything from high society to slaves in the cotton fields. A special treat is *On the Pulse of Morning*, along with other poems in this complete collection of Maya Angelou's published poems.

Copyright 1994, Random House.

Recordings

A Celebration with Maya Angelou, Guy Johnson and Janice Mirikitani

To celebrate Guy Johnson's 50th birthday, Dr. Angelou granted her son's request to read poetry with her. On September 9, 1995, at the Calvin Simmons Theater in Oakland, California, Angelou, Johnson, and Janice Mirikitani produced a recording of poetry readings.

Been Found

Nicholas ("Nick") Ashford and Valerie ("Val") Simpson, known as the popular R&B duo "Ashford and Simpson" were guests at Angelou's house one Thanksgiving. At Angelou's house in North Carolina, Nick Ashford played around on the piano and asked Angelou and Val Simpson to join him. Val Simpson took over on the piano, at Nick's prodding, and Angelou began talking to the music. Simultaneously, Nick Ashford ad-libbed on vocals. A cassette tape captured the moment. This was the beginning of the first song, *I Remember All*, on the 1996 *Been Found* album. Seven of the 11 songs feature Angelou speaking, with Ashford and Simpson singing.

Just Churchin'

Just Churchin' was recorded live in Nashville and Chicago. This powerful collection of 13 revered church selections was produced by Derek Lee. Dr. Maya Angelou makes a guest appearance on the traditional gospel hymn titled *Just a Closer Walk with Thee*. Dr. Angelou provides a commentary on the state of African-Americans on this rendition. Other artists who appeared on this recording were Vicki Winans, Vanessa Bell Armstrong, Donald Lawrence and James Moore. The project was released by Gospo Centric Records.

Miss Calypso

At 27, Angelou recorded *Miss Calypso* for the fledgling Liberty Records. Initially recorded in 1957, the album was reissued on CD in 1996.

The Maya Angelou Poetry Collection (Unabridged)

The Maya Angelou Poetry Collection (Unabridged) collection has over 100 unabridged poems, read by Angelou herself, from three of her previously published volumes. They include "Oh Pray My Wings Are Gonna Fit Me Well," "I Shall Not Be Moved" and "Just Give Me a Cool Drink of Water 'Fore I Diiie."

Audio Cassette; Random House, 1999.

The Voyage of the Amistad

The Voyage of the Amistad is Angelou's audio collection of lyrical and poetic renderings from the Steven Spielberg film titled *Amistad*. *Amistad* starred Morgan Freeman, Anthony Hopkins, Djimon Hounsou and Matthew McConaughey.

E.P. Dutton, 1997; Audiocassette ed. Penguin Audiobooks, 1997.

Study and Teaching

Bloom, Harold, Editor. *Maya Angelou (Modern Critical Views)*. Chelsea House Pub, New York, 1998.

Bloom, Harold and Angelou, Maya. *Maya Angelou: I Know Why the Caged Bird Sings (Modern Critical Interpretations Series)*. Philadelphia: Chelsea House Pub., 1998.

Brandes, Jay. *Maya Angelou: A Bibliography of Literary Criticism.*

Hagen, Lyman B. *Heart of a Woman, Mind of a Writer, and Soul of a Poet: A Critical Analysis of the Writings of Maya Angelou.* University Press of America in Lanham, Maryland, 1996.

I Know Why the Caged Bird Sings Notes. Paperback Cliffs Notes, 1993.

McPherson, Dolly A. *Order Out of Chaos: The Autobiographical Works of Maya Angelou.* Virago Press, New York, NY, 1992.

Wallace-Megna, Joanne. *Understanding I Know Why the Caged Bird Sings: A Student Casebook to Issues, Sources and Historical Documents.* Published in Westport, Connecticut, Greenwood, 1998.

Williams, Mary E. *Readings on Maya Angelou.* Hardcover, 1998, by the Greenwood Publishing Group, Greenhaven Press, San Diego, CA, 1997.

Television Productions

Afro-Americans in the Arts

Afro-Americans in the Arts, a PBS documentary, won Angelou the Golden Eagle Award.

All Day Long

Angelou wrote the screenplay and directed this film, in 1974, for the American Film Institute.

Imagine what a harmonious world it could be if every single person, both young and old shared a little of what he is good at doing.

QUINCY JONES

The ultimate of being successful is the luxury of giving yourself the time to do what you want to do.

LEOTYNE PRICE

With the Supremes I made so much money so fast all I wanted to do was buy clothes and pretty things. Now I'm comfortable with money and it's comfortable with me.

DIANA ROSS

I will never give in to old age until I become old. And I'm not old yet!

TINA TURNER

Angelou on Burns

Subsequent to achieving fame and while living in Arkansas, Angelou was captured by the work of Robert Burns. In honor of the bicentennial of his death, Angelou visited Burns' homeland in Scotland. In *Angelou on Burns*, Angelou chronicles her journey in Scotland and illustrates the parallels between Angelou and Burns in this documentary.

Black African Heritage Series

Angelou narrated *Black African Heritage Series*, a four-part series on the history, traditions, and culture of Africa and its people. Angelou joined Gordon Parks, Ossie Davis and Julian Bond as narrators. The series was released in 1972.

I Know Why the Caged Bird Sings

Angelou wrote the script and musical score from *I Know Why the Caged Bird Sings*, the first in her series of autobiographies (with Leona Thuna and Ralph B. Woolsley). The production appeared on national television in 1979 over CBS.

Madagascar: A World Apart

Madagascar: A World Apart is scheduled to air on PBS through the year 2001. Produced by Andrew Young and Susan Todd, the episode titled the same, provided historical data on the piece of land that separated from Africa 125 million years ago. Bob Gillespie of Oasis Recording engineered the voiceover session with Angelou. The series was voted the Best Limited Series, in 1997, at the Jackson Hole Wildlife Film Festival.

Roots

This famous television miniseries is an adaptation of Alex Haley's book titled *Roots*. In 1977, Angelou received a nomination for an Emmy Award for her portrayal of Nyo Boto, Kunta Kente's grandmother.

Sister, Sister

Broadcast in 1982 over NBC, *Sister Sister*, a dramatic television play written by Angelou, explores the lives of members of a middle-class African-American family.

The Inheritors

Angelou wrote *The Inheritors*, a television special on African-Americans in 1976.

The Legacy

In 1976, Angelou wrote *The Legacy*, a television special on African-Americans.

The Living Edens

At the studio of Oasis Recording, Angelou's voice served as a narrative backdrop for an episode of this PBS special. *The Living Edens* was produced by ABC/Kane and was a Reader's Digest World presentation.

The Slave Coast

In 1972, Angelou narrates an exploration documentary of the slave coast. An estimated 15 million people were enslaved and shipped to other lands between the 17th and 19th centuries. The production focuses on the Asante of Ghana, the Yoruba of Nigeria, the acrobatic Dan dancers of the Ivory Coast, and the women warriors of Dahomey.

Touched by an Angel

Dr. Angelou and Natalie Cole appeared on the 1998 "Reunion" episode of *Touched by an Angel*, a weekly television series. The episode appeared in the show's second season.

Theatrical Productions

Adjoa Amissah

Before leaving Ghana, West Africa, in 1966, Angelou wrote *Adjoa Amissah*, a two-act musical.

Ajax

Angelou adopted an adaptation of Sophocles' *Ajax* for this 1974 two-act drama. The production premiered in Los Angeles at the Mark Taper Forum.

And Still I Rise

Angelou's poem, *And Still I Rise*, in 1976 was adapted into a play. The play premiered in Winston-Salem, North Carolina, in the fall of 1992, and again in January 1993. *And Still I Rise* was also performed at the Ensemble Theatre in Oakland, California.

Black! Blues! Black!

Angelou narrated *Black! Blues! Black!*, a ten-part television production in 1968, on African traditions in American life.

Cabaret for Freedom

Cabaret for Freedom, an off-Broadway music revue, produced in 1960, was a benefit for the Southern Christian Leadership Conference. Angelou received recognition as producer, director and performer. The production was a collaborative effort with comedian Godfrey Cambridge at the New York's Village Gate.

Calypso Heatwave

Angelou appeared in this off-Broadway play in 1957.

Encounters

Angelou appeared in this play, which was first produced by the Center Theater Group in 1974. The production opened at the Mark Taper Forum.

Getting Up Stayed on My Mind

This production premiered Angelou in 1967.

Look Away

Look Away made its first debut on Broadway in 1973. In it, Angelou appeared as a dressmaker and confidante of the recently widowed first lady Mary Todd Lincoln, played by Geraldine Page. She received a Tony nomination for her performance.

Moon on a Rainbow Shawl

The inhabitants of a tenement in Trinidad were the focal point of Errol John's play titled *Moon on a Rainbow Shawl*. Angelou directed the production for Akuntunde Productions which opened in London, England, in 1987.

The Blacks

The Blacks opened at St. Mark's Playhouse on May 4, 1961, with an all-African-American cast. Angelou played the role of the Queen. The role focused on a white-masked African-American who reigned over and judged those beneath. At the end of the play, the feared and victimized African-American minority turned on their oppressors in a frenzy of hatred.

This production won the Obie Award in 1961 for the best off-Broadway play, American or foreign. After 1,272 performances, *The Blacks* closed production on May 24, 1964.

The Civil War (A Diary)

At the Alley Theater in Houston, Texas, the producers attempted to create a bridge between the worlds of popular music and theater. This attempt produced a theatrical concept recording of the Civil War which Atlantic Records released in January 1979. Musical guests included John Popper of Blues Traveler, Patti LaBelle, Bebe Winans, and Hootie and the Blowfish. James Garner, Charlie Daniels, Danny Glover, Ellen Burstyn and Dr. Maya Angelou also played major roles in this recording.

The Clawing Within

The Clawing Within was a two-act drama written by Angelou in 1966.

The Least of These

The Least of These was a two act drama produced by Angelou in 1955.

Works About the Author

Alden, Daisy. *In a Review of The Heart of a Woman.* World Literature Today, 1982.

Bell-Scott, Patricia. *Double-Stitch: Black Women Write About Mothers and Daughters.* Foreword by Maya Angelou, Beacon Press, Massachusetts, 1991.

Bloom, Lynn Z. *Maya Angelou 4 April 1928-. Dictionary of Literary Criticism.* Volume 38. Gale Research Company. 1985.

Blundell, Janet Boyarin. *In a Review of Shaker, Why Don't You Sing?* Library Journal, 1983.

Blundell, Janet Boyarin. *In a Review of The Heart of a Woman.* Publishers Weekly, 1981.

Braxton, Joanne M. *Maya Angelou 1928-. Modern American Women Writers.* Charles Scribner's Sons, 1991.

Casey, Ellen Miller. *In a Review The Heart of a Women.* Best Sellers, January, 1982.

Christian, Barbara T. Angelou. *Contemporary Authors.* New Revision Series. Volume 19. 1987.

Conway, Jill K. *Written by Herself: Autobiographies of American Women.* Vintage, 1992.

Cosgrave, Mary Silva. *In a Review of Shaker, Why Don't You Sing?* The Horn Book Magazine, 1983.

Courtney-Clarke, Margaret. *African Canvas: The Art of West African Women.* Foreword by Maya Angelou, Rizzoli International, New York City, 1991.

Freeman, Sharron. *In a Review of All God's Children Need Traveling Shoes.* Voice of Youth Advocates, 1986.

Gargan, Carol. *In a Review of And I Still Rise.* Best Sellers, 1979.

Gottlieb, Annie. Angelou. *Contemporary Authors.* New Revision Series. Volume 19, 1987.

Grumbach, Doris. *Maya Angelou 4 April 1928-. Contemporary Literary Criticism.* Gale Research Company. Volume 12, 1980.

Hinds, Patricia M., Editor. *ESSENCE: 25 Years Celebrating Black Women.* Foreword by Maya Angelou, Introduction by Susan L. Taylor. Essence Books.

Jelinke, Etelle C. *In Search of the African-American Female Self: African- American Women's Autobiographies and Ethnicity,* in Women's Autobiography, 1980.

Jordan, June. *Maya Angelou 4 April 1928.* Contemporary Literary Criticism. Gale Research Company. Volume 12, 1930.

Lanker, Brian. *I Dream a World: Portraits of Black Women Who Changed America.* Stewart Tabori & Cha, 1989.

Lewis, David Levering. *Maya Angelou: From Harlem to the Heart of a Woman.* Book World, The Washington Post, 1991.

Long, Richard A. *African Americans: A Portrait.* Foreword by Maya Angelou. Cresent Books, 1993.

McDowell, Deborah E. *Traveling Hopefully.* The Women's Review of Books, 1986.

MacKethan, Lucinda H. *Mother Wit: Humor in Afro-American Women's Autobiography.* Studies in American Humor, 1985.

Maddocks, Fiona. *In a Review of I Know Why the Caged Bird Sings.* New Statesman, 1984.

Miller, Adam David. *Angelou. Contemporary Authors.* New Revision Series. Volume 19, 1987.

Moore, Leonard D. *Review of I Shall Not Be Moved.* Library Journal, 1990.

Neubauer, Carol E. *Displacement and Autobiographical Style in Maya Angelou's The Heart of a Woman.* African-American Literature Forum, 1983.

Nilsen, Alleen P. *Maya Angelou 4 April 1928-.* Contemporary Literary Criticism. Gale Research Company. Volume 12, 1980.

Ott, Bill. *In a Review of The Heart of a Woman.* Booklist, 1981.

Phillips, Frank L. *Maya Angelou 4 April 1928-.* Contemporary Literary Criticism. Gale Research Company. Volume 12, 1980.

Silva, Candelaria. *In a Review of Shaker, Why Don't You Sing?* School Library Journal, 1983.

Smith, Sidonie Ann. *The Song of a Caged Bird: Maya Angelou's Quest After Self- Acceptance.* The Southern Humanities Review, 1973.

Smith, Sidonie Ann. *Maya Angelou 4 April 1928-.* Contemporary Literary Criticism. Gale Research Company. Volume 12, 1980.

Stepto, R.B. *The Phenomenal Woman and the Severed Daughter.* Parnassus: Poetry in Review. 1979.

Tate, Claudia. *African-American Writers at Work,* 1983.

Thurston, Zora N. *Dust Tracks on the Road: An Autobiography.* Foreword by Maya Angelou, HarperCollins, New York City, 1991.

America's Firsts

Ed Bradley, First and only African-American co-anchor of *60 Minutes*.

William Wells Brown wrote *Clotel* and became the first African-American to publish a black novel.

Alex Haley is the internationally known author of *Roots*. Haley is the first African American to win a Pulitzer prize for *Roots*.

Florence B. Price won recognition as a composer and is the first African-American to receive this honor.

Gwendolyn Brooks became the first African-American woman to win a Pulitzer prize for poetry.

Maya Angelou is considered the first African-American woman editor of an English language magazine for a foreign country.

Phillis Wheatley is one of the first African-American poets. In 1770, Ms. Wheatley became one of the earliest published African-American women writers.

Standing Among the Few Great Journalists

Angelou, Maya
    Baye, Betty
        Bradley, Ed
            Brown, Tony
                Douglass, Frederick
                    Griffin, Junius
                        Johnson, Robert E.
                        Jordan, Bob
                            Malloy, Courtland

Malveaux, Julianne
    McClain, Leanita
        Murray, Joan
            Page, Clarence
                Parks, Gordan
                    Raspberry, William
                        Reynolds, Barbara
                          Riley, Clayton
                            Robinson, Maxwell

Rowan, Carl T.
    Russwurm, John
        Shaw, Bernard
            Strait, George
                Tatum, James
                    Wells, Ida B.
                        Wickham, DeWayne

Standing Among the Few Great Luminaries of Literature

Adoff, Arnold
Ali, Shaharazad
Angelou, Maya
Baldwin, James
Barrett, Lindsay
Behn, Aphra
Bennett, Christine
Bennett, Gwendolyn
Bennett, Lerone
Bonner, Marita O.
Bontemps, Arna
Bourne, George
Boyd, Melba Joyce
Branch, Bruce W.
Brawley, Benjamin
Brown, Claude
Brown, Frank London
Brown, Sterling A.
Brown, William Wells
Bumbara, Toni Cade
Burroughs, Margaret
Butler, Octavia
Chestnutt, Charles
Churchill, Caryl
Clarke, John Henrik
Collier, Eugenia W.
Cotter, Joseph
Cullen, Countee
Davis, Allison
Davis, Arthur P.

Davis, John P.
Delany, Samuel R.
Demby, William
Douglass, Frederick
DuBois, W.E.B.
Dunbar-Nelson, Alice
Ellison, Ralph "Waldo"
Fauset, Jennie Redmon
Fisher, Rudolph
Fuller, Meta V.W.
Fuller, Hoyt
Furman, Abraham L.
Gaines, Ernest J.
Goodwin, Gail
Gordimer, Nadine
Graham, Lorenz
Graham, Effie
Granger, Robert
Hagen, Uta
Hairston, Loyle
Haley, Alex
Hamer, Martin J.
Hamilton, Virginia
Harper, Frances E.
Harper, Micheal S.
Himes, Chester
Hobbs, Avaneda
Hurston, Zora Neale
Jackson, Rebecca
Johnson, James Weldon

Johnson, Charles Richard
Jones, Bessie
Jones, Bill T.
Jordan, Jennifer
Kelley, William Melvin
Kincaid, Jamaica
Kingston, Maxine Hong
Lee, Audrey
Lincoln, Charles Eric
Lorde, Audre
Lyda, Wesley J.
Malveaux, Julianne
Marshall, Paule
Mason, Bobbie Ann
Matheus, John F.
Mathews, Charles
McCluskey, John
McMillan, Terry
McPherson, James
Meriwether, Louis
Millender, Dharathula
Moody, Anne
Morgan, Meli'sa
Morrison, Toni
Murray, Albert
Murray, James P.
Naylor, Gloria
Neal, Larry
Nichols, Grace
Njeri, Itabari
Offord, Carl Ruthven
Parker, Pat
Parker, Dorothy
Petry, Anne Lane
Plumpp, Sterling
Raboteau, Albert J.

Redding, Jay Saunders
Reed, Ishamael
Robeson, Paul
Robinson, Marilynne
Robotham, Rosemarie
Sanchez, Sonia
Saxton, Alexander P.
Scott, Ed Royal
Smith, Barbara
Smith, Ronald R.
Smith, John Caswell
Soyinka, Wole
Spencer, Anne
Stallworth, Anne Nall
Stickney, Yvonne
Styron, William
Taylor, Susan
Thomas, Joyce Carol
Thornbrough, Emma Lou
Toomer, Jean
Turner, Frederick W.
Van Peebles, Melvin
Vanzant, Iyanla
Vroman, Mary Elizabeth
Walker, Margaret
Walker, Alice
Wasserstein, Wendy
Welsing, Frances Cress
West, Dorothy
White, Lynn
White, Ellen Gould
Wideman, John Edgar
Williams, John Alfred
Wright, Jay
Wright, Richard
Yerby, Frank

Standing Among the Few Great Poets

Ada

Ai "Florence Anthony"

Angelou, Maya

Aubert, Alvin

Austin, Ramona

Brooks, Gwendolyn

Campbell, James Edwin

Chase-Riboud, Barbara S.

Clifton, Thelma Lucille

Cobb, Alice Spriggs

Cortez, Jayne

Cover, Jennifer

Danner, Margaret

Dove, Rita

Dunbar, Paul Lawrence

Evans, Mari

Giovanni, Nikki

Guillen, Nicolas

Hammon, Jupiter

Hantske, Madeline Horres

Hayden, Robert

Horton, George

Hughes, Langston

Johnson, Helene

Johnson, Georgia Douglas

Jones, Gayle

Kamunyakaa, Yusef

Knight, Ethridge

Kunjufu, Johari M. Amini

Madhubuti, Haki R.

Major, Clarence

Matthews, David

McKay, Claude

Miller, May

Moss, Thylias

Piercy, Marge

Pitts, Lucia M.

Plato, Ann

Rashad, Johari

Redmond, Eugene B.

Rodgers, Carolyn

Sarton, May

Terry, Lucy

Wheatley, Phyllis

Whitman, Alberry Allson

Only a generation of readers will span a generation of writers.

STEVEN SPIELBERG

FOR -

Not just talking the talk but for walking the walk, thank you.

Your sage counsel and endearing yourself to those who will led in generations to come, thank you.

Echoing life to a burdened soul, thank you.

Deciding to speak again, thank you.

Creating a better, more beautiful, more loving world for children and all humanity, thank you.

Lifting us through your words and passion, thank you.

Inspiring others to pursue their visions and artistic goals, thank you.

Not "sugar coating" your message but giving it to us in real terms, thank you.

Bringing comfort to the hurting and wisdom and light to the uncertain mind, thank you.

Your relentless wisdom that astonishes as well as gives us hope, thank you.

Taking us to the next level, thank you.

Allowing us to trace our own lives and to begin to appreciate, along with you, the agony of defeat, the pain of suffering, but the inevitable triumph in victory, thank you.

Being a part of the black voices of triumph throughout their struggle for excellence in the black community from the Jim Crow era to the present, thank you.

Reminding our people and the whole world that we are all cut from the same fabric of humanity, thank you.

Lending your great literary skills to the shaping of the social, political and economic consciousness of America, thank you.

Summing up Walt Disney's mission in building the Millennium Village, "world without borders," thank you.

Inspiring, teaching and enlightening our hearts, thank you.

Sending a message of peace, hope and inspiration to all, thank you.

Continuing to rise and impact America's society with the spirit of life, thank you.

Sparking a flame in our academic souls that has yet to perish, thank you.

Writing your way into the hearts of millions, thank you.

Using your words to touch countless lives and shape the destinies of so many people, both young and old, thank you.

Your unswerving devotion to human rights, your unwavering dedication to improving the lives of children worldwide, and your unstinting sharing of your enormous gifts on behalf of organizations and individuals in need, thank you.

Being a balm in America that has helped to make the wounded whole, thank you.

Being a mouthpiece for the dreams, aspirations, longings and relentless struggle of our community, thank you.

All you have done, we simply say thank you Dr. Maya Angelou, thank you.

Intimate Moments

America Speaks . . .

Dear Dr. Angelou:

I bring you greetings from Washington, D.C., the nation's capital. I have admired you for many years. When this opportunity was presented, my lips pronounced "yes" before the rest of me realized what I was doing. Sharing my thoughts with you in this letter is a dream come true. Having it published so everyone can see how I feel about you is even more exhilarating.

When God gave us you, Dr. Maya Angelou, he gave us his very best. But then, God does everything well. Even when we consider ourselves unworthy or lacking in anything, he still loves us and gives us his best. What's more inspiring, is that he will even send "messengers" along the way to encourage us . . . taking us to the next level. Thank God that he made you a conqueror over the most dismal circumstances. You have indeed passed the torch of caring, sharing and loving.

Phenomenal Woman means a lot to me. Though it's my favorite, I have read several of your other books. The words spoken and written on paper have given me direction. They have motivated me to pursue the very best life has to offer.

Thanks for inspiring and helping me. I will always be grateful and appreciative for the gift within you that was given. I bid you God's richest blessings as you continue to make a mark in life that can never be erased.

SHARON GOODMAN

★ ★ ★ ★ ★ ★

Dear Dr. Angelou:

Dr. Angelou, thank you for sharing your life's story with a sense of spirituality, warmth, compassion and humor. Through your writings you have shown me how to rejoice in pain, celebrate life through hardships and victories, and to sing in four-part rich harmony, the songs of praise with boldness. Above all, you have given me wisdom nuggets about how to deal with multifaceted life experiences.

After reading your material, whether it was poetry or a narrative about historical events, you wrote with such sensitivity in portraying the many obstacles Americans have faced over the decades. You have taken me out of my surroundings and caused me to travel with you in and out of various scenarios. By doing so, I traced my own life and began to appreciate, along with you, the agony of defeat, the pain of suffering, but the inevitable triumph in victory. God bless you always for helping me to triumph with you.

REV. DONNA W. BROWN

★ ★ ★ ★ ★ ★

Women of Destiny

Love International Church
6621-G Electronic Drive, Springfield, VA 22151-4302

Founder
Women of Destiny Ministries

Chaplain
WNBA Washington Mystics Basketball Association

Dear Dr. Maya Angelou:

The Women's Ministry of Love International Church, would like to thank you for your outstanding contributions made to women, children, minorities and communities.

You have significantly impacted and enhanced our lives in special ways. As a role model your life has shaped, directed and given insight to many of us, as you have allowed Christ Jesus to be Lord of your life. We gleam from your achievements that have inspired us to help reach our destiny.

On behalf of the Women of Destiny and generations of women to come who will find purpose and destiny through your legacy, again, we say thank you.

In His Service,

Rose M. Bonner
Co-Pastor

> If you view all the things that happen to you
> both good and bad, as opportunities,
> then you operate out of a
> higher level of consciousness.

LES BROWN

the orator

THE PASSION OF DR. MAYA ANGELOU'S WRITING HAS INSPIRED a nation. However, Angelou's depth goes beyond her literary works and presentations. Her presence, beauty, and masterful use of language creates a demand for her oratory. On stage, Maya Angelou electrifies an audience.

Angelou's voice has inspired millions because of her forthright outlook on life. Serving as a symbol of success, it is easy for America to listen to the voice that motivates and inspires. With intestinal fortitude, Maya Angelou courageously delivers facts instead of fiction. Having an orator-to-listener discussion with her audiences, Angelou articulates her heart and soul with creative ingenuity delineated with precision. Beginning from her childhood and progressing to adulthood, Dr. Angelou unabashedly shares her experiences on a multiplicity of topical areas. All viewpoints and comments come forth as unfolding mysteries that have been seasoned with time.

In this segment, you will learn where she has delivered some of her speeches, poems and made interesting statements. These presentations were given at various places throughout the United States.

50th Anniversary Celebration of the United Nations
On June 26, 1995, the United Nations celebrated the 50th Anniversary of the United Nations Charter with Dr. Maya Angelou as the keynote speaker. For the occasion, Dr. Angelou wrote a poem titled *The Brave and Startling Truth*.

Body and Soul Conference
Angelou was one of the keynote speakers at the Body and Soul conference that focused on alternative health remedies. Other featured speakers for the conference included Bernie Siegel, Matthew Fox, Shakfi Gowain, Terence McKenna and James Redfield. The conference was held from October 31 through November 2, 1997.

141

EMBRACED

BY A NATION

President William Jefferson Clinton embraces Dr. Maya Angelou after she recited *On the Pulse of the Morning* at his 1993 Presidential inauguration.

Michigan State University

At the 1990 Celebrity Lecture Series at Michigan State University, Maya Angelou was one of the keynote speakers. Angelou held the audience spellbound with stories of her childhood. Her oratorical presentation ranged from story to poem to song and back again. However, her theme was love and the universality of all lives. She read excerpts from poems of several African-American writers such as James Weldon Johnson and Paul Laurence Dunbar. Angelou also expressed her love for William Shakespeare's works.

"The honorary duty of a human being is to love," said Angelou. Quoting from her own work, she said "I am human and nothing human can be alien to me."

Million Man March

On October 3, 1996, leaders of the Million Man March asked one woman and only one woman to speak to the masses. That woman was Maya Angelou. For this brief moment in African-American history, Maya Angelou looked out among the million black men who assembled that day in Washington, D.C. Angelou's voice reverberated with power and truth. The world listened to her with compassionate hearts as she presented a powerful and life changing message. A special poem was written for the March and it was read into the hearing of many, who listened attentively to America's matriarch.

Million Woman March

The Million Woman March was held one year from the Million Man March in Washington, D.C. On October 25, 1997, in Philadelphia, Pennsylvania, several African-American personalities were available for this momentous occasion. Angelou, one of the featured orators, encouraged women to begin helping themselves.

Presidential Inauguration

Dr. Angelou is the first African-American female and the second poet asked to read a poem at the inauguration of a United States president. The first was Robert Frost, who spoke at the inauguration of President John Kennedy in 1960. *On the Pulse of Morning* was read by Dr. Angelou, before millions of viewers, after President William Jefferson Clinton was sworn in. This was a crowning moment of achievement for her. Eloquently delivered, Dr. Maya Angelou recited her poetic masterpiece with grace and style.

Rev. Dr. Martin Luther King, Jr.'s 1990 Birthday Celebration

Dr. Angelou was a keynote speaker at the 1990 Rev. Dr. Martin Luther King, Jr.'s birthday celebration in High Point, North Carolina. In that speech, Angelou shared the importance of remembering leaders who gave their lives to advance humanitarian causes.

One specific analogy she used focused was on why African-Americans endured hardships — specifically physical abuse. Angelou said they did so to stay employed and to afford their children with the privilege of attending America's premier colleges and universities.

Shaw University

Nearly 1,000 people gathered at Raleigh Memorial Auditorium on November 21, 1997, for the kickoff of Shaw University's homecoming weekend. Angelou, the keynote speaker, recited poetry and entertained the audience. Urging the attendees to "go to the library," Angelou reminded the young men and women that roads to success for them had already been "paid for." She also told them, "Your inheritance is so incredibly rich. Poetry has a way of allowing you to heal yourself. Since life is our most precious gift, let's make sure that our conscious life is dedicated to the liberation of the human mind and spirit, beginning with your own."

Sweet Briar College

Overflow crowds packed the Babcock Auditorium of Sweet Briar College on Wednesday, November 5, 1998. Students and community members swarmed to hear the renowned poet. Many of them waited three hours in line just to sit near the podium. The Director of Communications, Dave Blount, stated that Maya Angelou was requested by the students and on the top of their wish list.

To accommodate the overflow crowds and allow everyone to see one of the greatest voices of contemporary literature, the school's officials provided video linkups to the Wailes Student Center and Prothro Commons. Angelou, who had not been to Central Virginia in 20 years, said "My hope is to be an inspiration to young men and women and to teach them to risk losing their ignorance." Dr. Angelou also spoke about poetry as a "rainbow in the clouds." Angelou recited and sang many of her poems.

The Distinguished Annie Clark Tanner Lecture

On May 8, 1997, Dr. Maya Angelou spoke at Weber State University for the 16th-Annual Families Alive Conference. Angelou reminded the attendees that "When it looked like the sun wasn't going to shine anymore, God put a rainbow in the clouds." Riveted by this great orator of contemporary literature, the audience listened intently as Angelou articulated the struggles of African-Americans while describing the omnipotence of God to change dire circumstances. Dr. Angelou said, "Ms. Rosie, when I see you through your devotion, through your tenderness, your love, your mercy, I stand up, and I realize when it looked like the sun wasn't going to shine anymore, you and you and you and you became a rainbow in the clouds."

University of Delaware's 147th Commencement Ceremony

The University of Delaware's 147th Commencement Ceremony was attended by more than 25,000 graduates and family and friends. This was the largest crowd ever in the university's history. Standing before a hushed and attentive crowd, Angelou sang out, "When it looked like the sun wasn't gonna to shine anymore, God put a rainbow in the sky." Fusing history with poetry, Dr. Angelou encouraged the young men and women, whom she said had already been paid for. She said, "In any case, where you will be greatest, the areas in which you will be the most important will be the areas in which you inspire, encourage and support another human being." Dr. Angelou concluded her speech to the Class of 1996 with a poem, titled *A Brave and Startling Truth*, which she wrote for the United Nations 50th Anniversary Celebration in 1995.

Worldfest 1996

Worldfest is a week-long celebration of international cultures at the University of Cincinnati. In 1996, the theme was "Celebrating a Caring Community of Cultures." Many participants attended a session titled "An Afternoon with Maya Angelou" on Wednesday, May 1, 1996.

Take this kiss upon the brow!
And, in parting from you now,
This much let me avow —
You are not wrong who deem
That my days have been a dream;
Yet if hope has flown away
In a night, or in a day,
In a vision, or in none,
Is it therefore the less gone?
All that we see or seem
Is but a dream within a dream.

EDGAR ALLAN POE

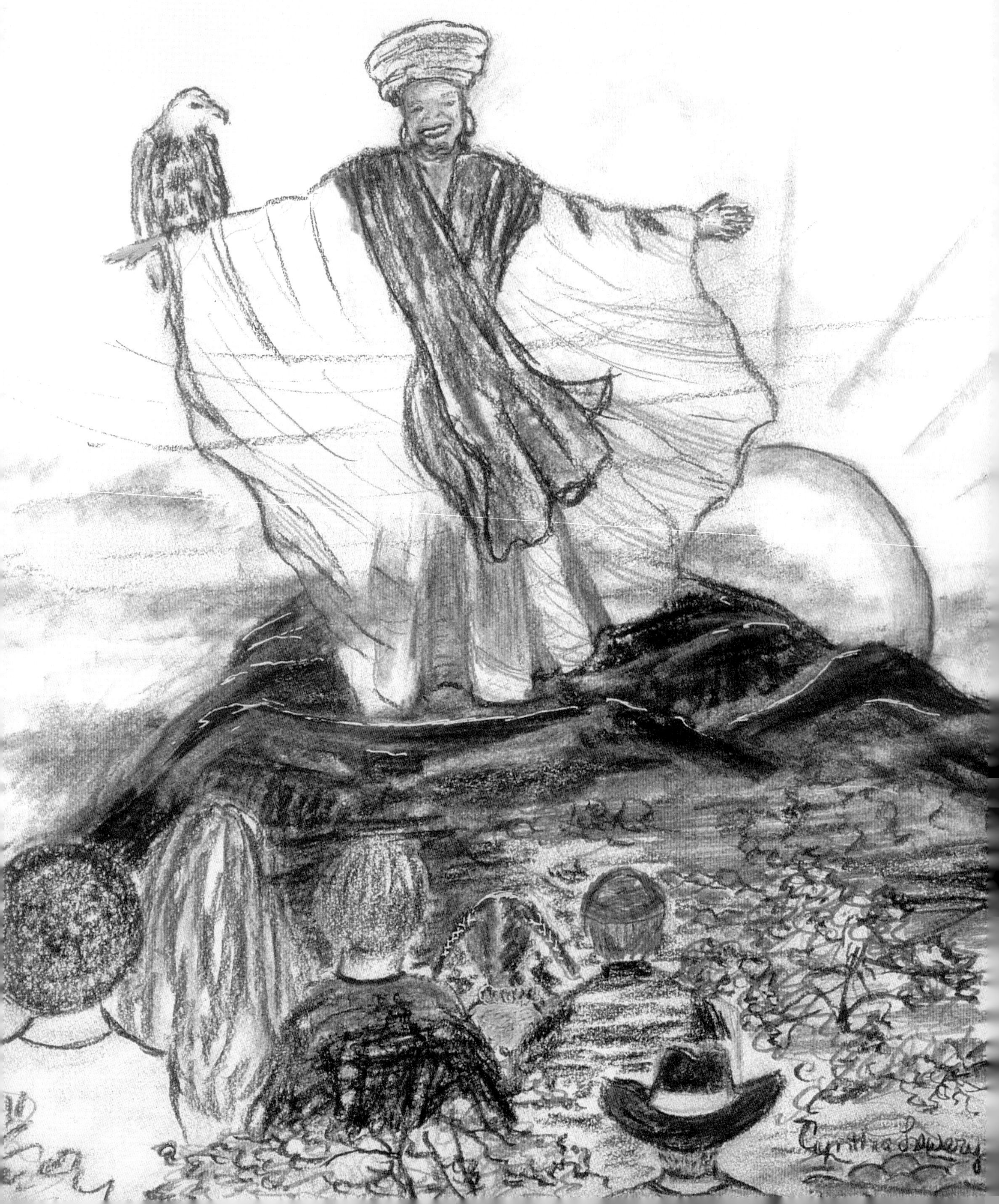
Cynthia Lowery

Intimate Moments

THE POTTER'S HOUSE

6777 W. Kiest
Boulevard.
Dallas,
TX
75236
•
214 331-0954
Voice
•
214 337-5375
Fax
•

Maya Angelou, a friend to her community, is a mouthpiece for the dreams, aspirations, longings and relentless struggle of our community. Her words echo not from the pulpit or political soapbox like so many of the other generations of leaders who have made their mark. But, her words come from the pen of the poet, the author and thinker. A searcher of the hearts of men, she is well acquainted with the cry of the human heart, and the paths of life that lead to resolve, and hope and release from the contradictions inherent in human existence.

My congratulations are with you. Your ideas have birthed words, and your words have formed new ideas about life in those who have partaken of your musings. Your words and ideas have substantially benefited our world in spheres as diverse as education and philanthropy and religion and theatre. Dr. Angelou, I celebrate your life, I honor your gift, and I thank God for a fellow wordsmith with a message that has touched and challenged uncounted millions.

Sincerely,

Bishop Thomas D. Jakes

Bishop T.D. Jakes, Sr.
Founder/CEO
The Potter's House/T.D. Jakes Ministries

Bishop
T.D. Jakes,
Pastor
Founder

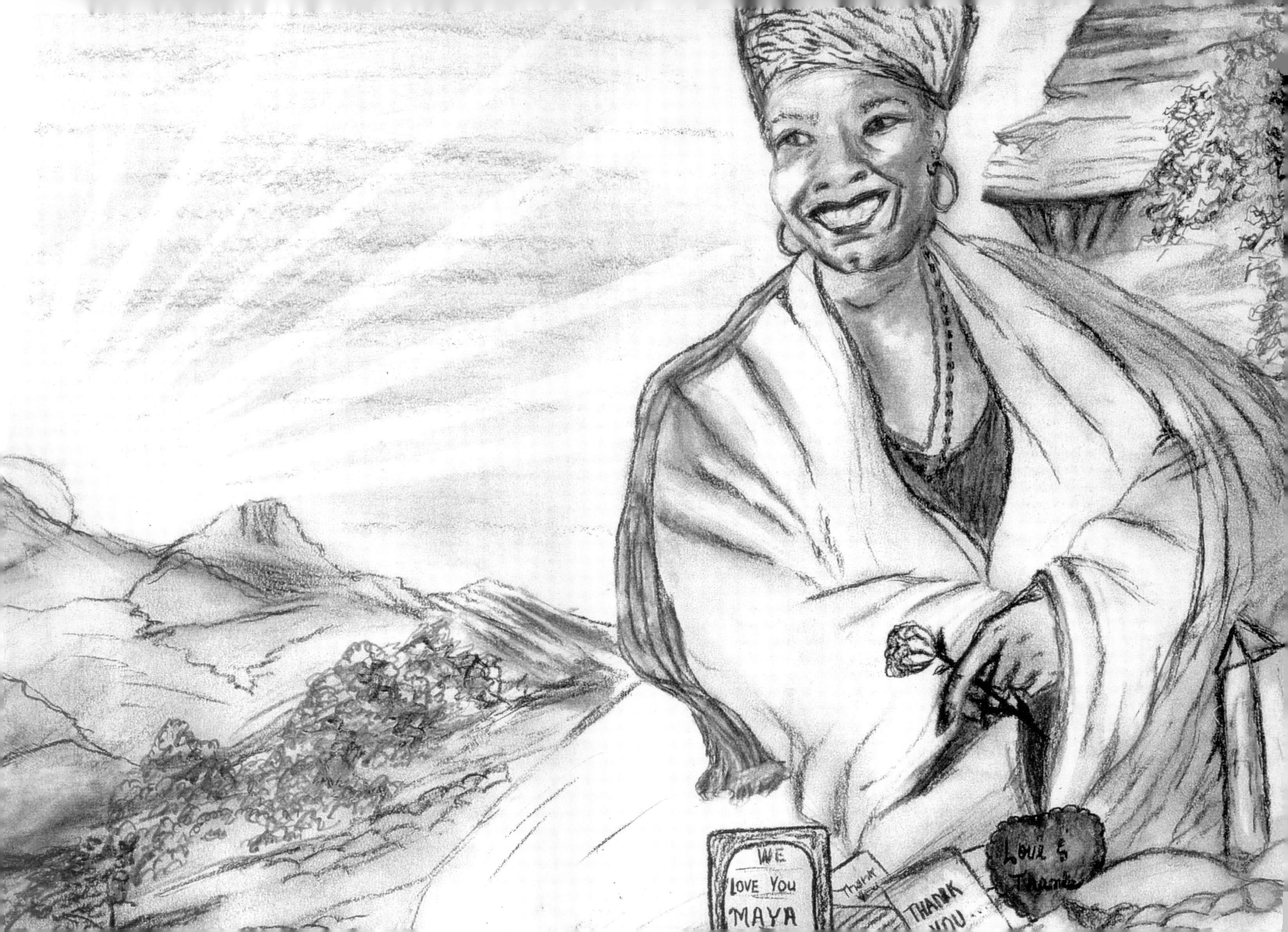
WE
LOVE YOU
MAYA
THANK YOU
Love &
Thanks

A Little Texas Entertainment Co.

P.O. Box 7000 • Dallas, TX 75209

Dear Dr. Angelou:

It is with extreme pleasure that I write a congratulatory letter acknowledging your inimitable literary contributions to the people of God's nation. As a small girl, the first novel I ever read was *I Know Why The Caged Bird Sings*. Your triumph over silence, as well as your insatiable desire to learn, sparked a flame in my academic soul that has yet to perish.

I have shared your biography as a gift with each of my nieces. I feel it is my duty to share such a great literary work with every young girl I am blessed to be more than acquaintances with. I really do not have the words to express what your talent means to me. By now and based on this nation's responses to you, I am certain you have some idea.

Thank you for deciding to speak again. Your voice is melodious. And thank you for writing your way into the hearts of millions.

I Remain Sincere,

Dr. Micaela Dartson, CEO

NEW BETHEL WORLD BIBLEWAY CME CHURCH
410 Reese Street
Sandusky, Ohio 44870-3755
(419) 626-4833 (Office)

Dear Dr. Angelou:

Greetings in the name of our people, the Creator of the universe, and our ancestors. I hope that this letter finds you in good health and spirits.

I am writing this letter to you as a personal testimony of how you have touched my life in so many ways. I want you to know just how much your life and your accomplishments have meant to my life.

First, when I read your autobiography, *I Know Why The Caged Bird Sings,* I was awed at your many and varied accomplishments. I am humbled by your experiences and I am emotionally overjoyed and stimulated by your poetry. God reveals to me the nature of an individual who is seeking to follow the Creator and to do his will no matter what the venue.

You are a poet, author, actress, singer, playwright, and a historian. It does not matter where the Creator leads you, you just go. Like a prophet of God who speaks "Thus Saith the Lord," you portray His essence, love, and beauty through the many tools that he has embodied in you. Namely, the words that he has inspired you to write.

You truly have and are continuing to realize the potential that the Creator has given you. Dr. Angelou, that example continues to inspire me. I, too, find myself contributing to the world in many different ways. I do not limit myself to any one field or any one set of circumstances. I just allow the Creator to work through me as "He sees fit." I do not worry about the criticisms, but am compelled to keep on moving as the Creator would have me do. With this, I hope and seek to realize my full potential. Your life and your testimony keep me going and pushing on toward God's will for my life. When I see an example, such as yours, I know that I am on the right track and I know that there is a Creator who loves me.

Second, I am a man who loves young people. I authored a book titled *Reviving Our Youth.* It looks at a number of reasons why youths, between the ages of 12 and 17, might be alienated from the African-American church. I want you to know that your poem titled *The Black Family Pledge* deeply moved me in the spirit. That masterpiece is appreciated very much because of the way you remembered our African tribal past and the ancestors who are an intricate part of the African religious belief system. You say that because we have forgotten our past, and I interpret "we" to mean "parents or the community of parenting," our children are suffering and decaying. They are doing so right in front of us. You called us back to our ancestry and back to our brotherhood and sisterhood because "we are our brothers and sisters." I deeply appreciate the call back.

In closing, I just wanted to say that your life is a wonderful testimony for men and women alike regardless of race, creed or color. Personally, I will continue to be moved by your poems, your artistry and your life. Dr. Maya Angelou, you are truly a "phenomenal woman." Thank you for being such a great inspiration.

In the name of our people, the Creator of the universe, and our ancestors,

Dr. Eddie L. Grays, Jr., Pastor
Professor of Religion, Cleveland State University

*If you haven't got any charity in your heart,
you have the worst kind of heart trouble.*

BOB HOPE

the humanitarian

DR. MAYA ANGELOU IS ONE OF OUR NATION'S GREATEST humanitarians. The champion of many worthwhile causes, Angelou has raised millions of dollars for worthwhile charities. It would be impossible to list the countless causes for which she has made contributions. However, listed below are a few of her philanthropical bestowals.

A Celebration with Maya Angelou, Guy Johnson and Janice Mirikitani

To celebrate Guy Johnson's 50th birthday, Dr. Angelou granted her son's request to read poetry with her. On September 9, 1995, at the Calvin Simmons Theater in Oakland, California, Angelou, Johnson, and Janice Mirikitani produced a recording of poetry readings. Mirikitani is a third generation Japanese-American and a well-known poet, activist and choreographer. The project was a benefit to Project Open Hand and the National Poetry Association.

Black Film Center/Archive

The Black Film Center/Archive houses a collection of films and associated documentation and materials that depict some aspect of the African-American experience. The repository contains films by which African-Americans have made substantial contributions as writers, producers, directors, actors, musicians and consultants. Located on the Indiana University Bloomington campus, the facility allows scholars, researchers, and students to study, view, and have access to these materials for various purposes. The Black Film Center/Archive also produces a newsletter that serves as a community, academic and professional resource.

Dr. Angelou is one of the sponsors for the organization. As a sponsor, Angelou helps to raise funds to help support the organization's goals and objectives. Other African-American sponsors include actors Harry Belafonte, Donald Bogle, Pearl Bowser, George Stanford Brown, Charles Burnett, Bernie Casey, Bill Cosby, Sidney Poitier, Quincy Jones, Robert Hooks and others.

Children's Defense Fund

In 1998, the Children's Defense Fund celebrated its 25th anniversary. Part of the festivities included a "Beat the Odds Celebration and Benefit." On Wednesday, March 25, 1998, at the Los Angeles Convention Center, a special tribute evening was held for musician Quincy Jones. The benefit was also to highlight the achievements of Los Angeles area high school students who had successfully completed the "Beat the Odds" program. The evening's program was hosted by author Maya Angelou.

Since 1990, the Children's Defense Fund has honored remarkable young people who have beaten incredible odds to succeed. The Children's Defense Fund has developed a "Beat the Odds" organizing manual to help many communities develop their own "Beat the Odds" celebrations. Cities involved in the program include Los Angeles, Atlanta, New York City, Minneapolis, the District of Columbia and East St. Louis.

Donations from the function were used to benefit the Children's Defense Fund Annual National Conference. Proceeds were matched by the Charles Stewart Mott Foundation and the Ford Foundation.

Hampton University

In October 1998, Hampton University's Ogden Hall was filled with the sounds of Angelou's rich voice. Center stage, Angelou shared words of wisdom while finger-snapping and hip-shaking. Though Angelou said that "we live in relation to our heroes," many college students present held Angelou as their "sheroe." Angelou gave this performance to help Hampton University's President William R. Harvey lead the school on a $200 million capital campaign.

Maya Angelou Elementary School

On December 15, 1995, Maya Angelou addressed students and faculty at the dedication of an elementary school in her name in Miami, Florida. The school opened in the fall of 1995 as a Saturn Project School with an emphasis in writing. School Board Member Frederica Wilson, Principal Maria B. Diaz, Region IV Superintendent Carol Cortez, and School Board Superintendent Octavio Viciedo were part of the ribbon cutting ceremony.

There are no secrets to success. It is the result of preparation, hard work, learning from failure.

GENERAL COLIN POWELL

Think not forever of yourselves, O Chiefs, nor of your own generation. Think of continuing generations of our families, think of our grandchildren and of those yet unborn, whose faces are coming from beneath the ground.

T.S. ELIOT

Maya Angelou Project

The Maya Angelou Project started as a comprehensive strategy for urban renewal to leverage broad community revitalization in the Boise neighborhood, in the inner North/Northeast section of Portland, Oregon. The project began with the renovation of an apartment complex, which was a well-known haven for drug and gang activity in Portland. Community residents, public agencies, and Housing Our Families, formed a partnership to manage the responsibilities of designing and carrying out the project. The project has been extremely successful and has influenced the transformation of an entire neighborhood.

Leaders credit the success of the project to over 200 community participants, who developed the Maya Angelou Community Initiative Project. The participants identified the neighborhood's needs, ranked those needs and developed the strategies to carry out the necessary changes to meet the needs. Paint-a-thons, home repair, clean ups, block watches, and neighborhood parties were some tools used by neighborhood residents to bring about a change.

Maya Angelou Raises Cash For Burned Churches

Angelou held a fundraiser at Mt. Zion Baptist Church, her home church in Winston-Salem, North Carolina. The Friday service's theme was "A Healing Time, A Healing Place."

The Associated Press issued a release over the wire, on November 24, 1996, about fundraising ventures being undertaken to help African-American churches. It stated that poet Maya Angelou and actor Ossie Davis were helping to raise money and awareness for churches burned by arsonists.

Angelou said, "People are already starting to forget the tragedies, which isn't necessarily a good thing." Angelou also said, "That is symptomatic of what is festering in our society…We are obliged to try to root out that fatal illness, ailment, disease, which has affected us." The Associated Press reported that many churches had no fire insurance, and some were having difficulty collecting on insurance policies. It was further reported that some insurance companies had canceled some church policies.

National Council of Churches of Christ of the USA

Local church leaders were joined by the National Council of Churches of Christ to remind President Clinton that the United States has a moral responsibility to fight global warming. The leaders believe the deterioration of our plant has become a moral issue. The National Council of Churches released a new global warming public service announcement narrated by Maya Angelou. In the 30-second TV spot, Angelou reminds us that "we are called to protect [the earth] so that we and our descendants may live."

National Society for the Prevention of Cruelty to Children and The National Deaf Children's Society

The National Society for the Prevention of Cruelty to Children and The National Deaf Children's Society launched a national helpline called "A Voice for Deaf Children." These two formidable companies launched "A Voice For Deaf Children" and "Safe In Your Hands," on Thursday, April 30, 1998, in the presence of Dr. Maya Angelou. The event took place at the Maya Angelou Child Protection Team and Family Centre in London, England.

Along with the helpline is an information pack, "Safe In Your Hands," for professionals who work with deaf children. The advice line and resource packet provides practical advice to help protect deaf children from emotional, physical, and sexual abuse and neglect.

See Forever

See Forever is designed to bring positive changes in the futures of young people. The program focuses on helping youths that had previously been involved in the juvenile justice system. Most are considered at risk of becoming career criminals.

Training opportunities are afforded the students who are serious about changing their lives and getting the skills necessary to do so. For example, students gain critical employment skills while working at a nonprofit restaurant called "Untouchable Taste Catering." The student technology center also helps students to gain additional experience. Programs at these outreaches are through three to four week internships throughout the year. Students are also required to attend the Maya Angelou Charter School. The schools maintain year-round and 11 hour-a-day schedules.

See Forever was founded by Assistant Attorney General Eric Holder and Attorney Reid Weingarten, and is run by David Domenici and James Forman, Jr. The advisory board includes Maya Angelou, Alma Brown, Robert Strauss, John Payton, and Jo-Ann Wallace. Supporters for the program include Mobil Oil, Kodak, IBM, the Soros Foundation, Fannie Mae Foundation, the Public Welfare Foundation, the Eugene Agnes Meyer Foundation, the Morris Gwendolyn Cafritz Foundation and George Washington University.

Special Olympics North Carolina Brookhill Gala

The Brookhill Steeplechase, sponsored by the Raleigh Jaycees, was the focal point of the third annual Brookhill Gala hosted by the Special Olympics North Carolina, on April 30, 1999. The Special Olympics North Carolina was led by Dr. Maya Angelou, the organization's honorary chairperson and keynote speaker. Dr. Angelou shared her many talents with the guests during the event, which were days and nights filled with music, dancing and entertainment. The festivities took place at the Raleigh City Museum, in the beautifully restored Briggs Hardware Building, located in downtown Raleigh, North Carolina. Other highlights of the Gala were live entertainment, special guest appearances and a live auction.

Seven thousand athletes, with mental retardation, represented over 150 countries and competed at the 1999 Special Olympics World Summer Games held in the Triangle area on June 26-July 4, 1999. The Special Olympics North Carolina was the largest sporting event held in North Carolina's history. Proceeds from the 1999 Brookhill Gala benefited the North Carolinian athletes, who was the largest delegation to compete in the 1999 Special Olympics World Summer Games.

Sri Chinmoy Oneness-Home Peace Run

Historically, the Sri Chinmoy Oneness-Home Peace Run is the longest relay run for peace. Held every two years, the organization invites participants, from over 100 nations, to take a step toward peace by carrying the "Peace Torch." The thrust is to help promote inspiration, friendship and hope. For those who have run in the relay, hearts and attitudes have been changed. In addition, those who have encouraged the runners have also experienced similar results. Major participants for this cause included Dr. Maya Angelou, Carl Lewis, Mother Teresa, Paul and Linda McCarthy, Muhammad Ali, Arnold Schwarzenegger and a host of others.

The Middle East Children's Alliance

The Middle East Children's Alliance uses its programs to help empower communities and to ensure the human rights of all people, especially children. Since 1988, the Middle East Children's Alliance has worked diligently to stop children from suffering. Other objectives of the agency are to educate Americans on U.S. and Middle East foreign policy. Regionally, the agency primarily focuses on those living in Palestine, Israel, Lebanon and Iraq. Many celebrities have supported the organization's causes. Some of them include actors Bernie Sanders, June Jordan, Richie Havens, Allen Ginsberg and Martin Sheen, and many others. More than $5 million worth of medicine, toys, food, and children's books have been delivered to children in the West Bank and Gaza Strip, in Lebanon and in Iraq.

Dr. Maya Angelou is a member of the Advisory Board for The Middle East Children's Alliance. The agency is located in Berkeley, California, and is a nongovernmental agency.

There is a Moral To It All

Don't Quit Your Day Job Records got together with Dr. Angelou and Jessica Mitford to

You can do what you have to do, and sometimes you can do it even better than you think you can.

FORMER PRESIDENT JIMMY CARTER

Every new idea is an impossibility until it is born.

FORMER SECRETARY OF COMMERCE RONALD BROWN

capture the essence of love both shared when entertaining at parties. Both legends would sing songs around the piano at parties. When asked to record by media escort Kathi Goldmark, Dr. Angelou replied with "Monday's good." Thus, a recording. Proceeds from the sales of the recording were donated to the Right to Rock Network and other First Amendment advocates.

Winston-Salem State University — The Maya Angelou National Institute for the Improvement of Child and Family Education

Winston-Salem State University has created an institute to help families take a proactive approach to helping children become productive citizens. The Institute is developing a model that will help the university play a major role on child development issues and in developing strong family support systems. The model will support the value of education, self-esteem and family support. Dr. Maya Angelou played a critical role in helping the university to establish this program.

America's Firsts

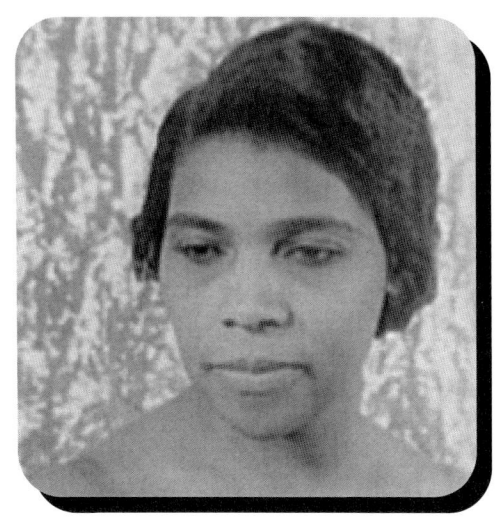

Marian Anderson is the first African-American to sing a leading role at the Metropolitan Opera in New York City.

Ella Fitzgerald is known as the first African-American "Lady of Song."

Mary Lou Williams is the first African-American "Lady of Jazz."

Shirley Chisholm was elected the first African-American congresswoman in 1968. In 1972, Ms. Chisholm became the first African-American to run for President.

Carol Moseley-Braun is the first African-American female and first African-American Democrat to be elected to the United States Senate.

Sharon Pratt-Kelly became the first African-American woman mayor of Washington, D.C., a major city.

L. Douglas Wilder was elected as the first African-American governor of Virginia and the first African-American elected as governor of any state.

Standing Among the Few Great Politicians

Angelou, Maya
Barry, Marion S.
Blackwell, Unita
Bond, Julian
Bradley, Tom
Braun, Carol Mosely
Brooke, Edward W.
Brown, Benjamin D.
Brown, Willie L.
Brown, Ronald
Bruce, Blanche K.
Bunche, Ralph J.
Burke, Yvonne Brathwaite
Burrs, Leslie
Chisholm, Shirley
Daley, Richard
Dellums, Ronald V.
DePriest, Oscar
Diggs, Charles, Jr.
Dinkins, David
Dixon, Sharon Pratt
Evers, Charles
Fauntroy, Walter E.
Ford, Harold
Gantt, Harvey
Gibson, Kenneth Allen

Gray, William
Harris, Patricia Roberts
Hatcher, Richard G.
Jackson, Jesse
Jackson, Maynard
Jordan, Barbara C.
Leidesdortt, William Alexander
Leland, Mickey
Mfume, Kweisi
Newhouse, Richard H.
Norton, Eleanor Holmes
Parker-Sawyer, Paula
Perkins, Edward J.
Pinchback, P.B.S.
Powell, Colin L.
Powell, Adam Clayton
Rangel, Charles
Savage, Gus
Stokes, Louis
Sullivan, Dr. Louis
Washington, Walter E.
Waters, Maxine
Wilder, L. Douglas
Williams, Polly
Young, Andrew
Young, Coleman

Standing Among the Few Great Musicians, Singers and Entertainers

Adams, Oleta
Adderley, Julian "Cannonball"
Albright, Gerald
Allen, Byron
Allen, Geri
Anderson, Thomas
Anderson, Marian
Angelou, Maya
Armatrading, Joan
Armstrong, Louis
Armstrong, Howard
Armstrong-Bell, Vanessa
Ashford, Nicholas
Austin, Patti
Aweke, Aster
Ayers, Roy
Badu, Erica
Baker, Anita
Baker, Josephine
Baker, David
Barron, Bill
Basie, William "Count"
Bass, Charlotta A.
Battle, Kathleen
Bechet, Sidney
Belle, Regina
Benson, George
Bernhardt, Clyde
Berry, Chuck
Beverly, Frankie

Blake, Eubie
Blakey, Art
Blige, Mary
Bofill, Angela
Boyz II Men
Brandy
Braxton, Toni
Bricktop, Ada Beatrice
Brooks, Lonnie
Brown, Ruth
Brown, Ray
Brown, Bobby
Brown, James
Brown, Clarence Gatemouth
Brown, Angela
Brubeck, Dave
Bumbry, Grace
Burnim, Mellonee V.
Burrows, Vinie
Butler, Jerry
Byrd, Donald
Calloway, Cab
Campbell, Tevin
Carey, Mariah
Carrington, Terri Lyne
Carter, Nell
Ceasar, Shirley
Chapman, Tracy
Charles, Ray
Chenier, Clifton

Cherry, Neneh
Chiffons
Chucky Duck
Clayton, John Jr.
Cleveland, James
Clifford, Linda
Coasters
Coe, Jimmy
Cole, Natalie
Cole, Nat King
Collins, Albert
Coltrane, John
Crawford, Beverly
Cray, Robert
Crouch, Andrae
Daniels, Billy
Darnell, August
Davis, Miles
Davis, Ossie/Ruby Dee
Davis, Anthony
Davy, Gloria
DeFranco, Buddy
Dibango, Manu
Diddley, Bo
Dirty Dozen Band
Domino, Antoine "Fats"
Dorsey, Thomas A.
Dream Girls
DuBois, Shirley
Duncan, Todd
Dynamics
Earth, Wind, and Fire
Eckstein, Billy
Edmonds, "Babyface"
Eldridge, Roy
Ellington, E. "Duke"
Falana, Lola

Fitzgerald, Ella
Flack, Roberta
Flavor Flav
Franklin, Aretha
Garrett, Kenny
Gaye, Marvin
Gill, Johnny
Gillespie, Dizzy
Grandy, Erroll
Gray, Denise
Green, Al
Greenfield, Elizabeth
Hakim, Talib Rasul
Hall, Danniebelle
Hamilton, Chico
Hammer, M.C.
Hampton Sisters
Hampton, Lionel
Hancock, Herbie
Harper Brothers
Havens, Richie
Hawkins, Walter
Hawkins, Edwin
Hawkins, Tramaine
Hayes, Roland
Hayes, Isaac
Heard, J.C.
Hill, Lauryn
Hinton, Milt
Holiday, Billie
Holiday, Jennifer
Hooker, John Lee
Horne, Lena
Houston, Whitney
Houston, Sissy
Hyman, Phyllis
Ice Cube

Ink Spots
Inner Circle
Isley Brothers
Jackson 5
Jackson, Freddie
Jackson, Isaiah
Jackson, Janet
Jackson, Mahalia
Jackson, Marlon
Jackson, Michael
Jackson, Milt
Jenkins, Tomi
Jessye, Eva
Johnson, James P.
Johnson, J.J.
Johnson, Robert
Jones, Quincy
Jones, Bobby
Joplin, Scott
Jordan, Louis
Kane, Big Daddy
Kendricks, Eddie
Khan, Chaka
King, B.B.
Knight, Gladys
Kool and the Gang
Kris Kross
LaBelle, Patti
Little, Richard
Living Colour
Love, Earl
Makeba, Miriam
Marley, Bob
Marsalis, Branford
Marsalis, Wynton
Martin, Sallie
Mathis, Johnny

Maultsby, Portia
Maze
McRae, Carmen
Memphis Slim
Mills, Stephanie
Mills Brothers
Mills, Florence
Monk, Thelonius
Moore, Undine Smith
Moore, Melba
Morgan, Frank
Nevilles
New Edition
Norman, Jessye
Nortorius B.I.G.
O'Jays
Ocean, Billy
Oliver, Joseph K.
Paris, Mica
Parker, Charlie
Person, Houston
Peterson, Oscar
Pickett, Wilson
Pointer Sisters
Price, Leontyne
Pride, Charley
Prince
Queen Latifah
Rainey, "Ma"
Rawls, Lou
Redd, Freddie
Reese, Della
Reeves, Martha
Richie, Lionel
Ricks, Valerie
Ripperton, Minnie
Roberts, Marcus

Robinson, Smokey
Ross, Diana
Ruffin, David
Rushen, Patrice
Rustin, Bayers
Sade
Scott, Michael
Shakur, Tupac
Simmons, Russel
Simone, Nina
Snow, Valaida
Spinners
Staple Singers
Sullivan, Maxine
Sumlin, Hubert
Summer, Donna
Sun Ra
Supremes
Sure, Al B.
Surface
Sweat, Keith
Sweet Honey
Sylvers
Take Six
Taliefero, Crystal
Tatum, Art
Taylor, Koko
Taylor, Billy
Temptations
Turner, Ike
Turner, Tina
Two Live Crew
Uggams, Leslie
Vandross, Luther
Vaughan, Sarah
Vaughan, Stevie Ray
Vaughan, Jimmy

Walden, Narada
Walker, Anita
Warfield, William
Warren, Mervyn
Warwick, Dionne
Washington, Grover
Washington, Dinah
Waters, Muddy
Waters, Ethel
Watley, Jody
Watson, Johnny
Watts, Andre
Weathers, Felicia
Webster, Katie
Wells, Mary
White, Barry
White, Josh
White, Doyle
Whitelowe, Helen
Whitfield, Thomas
Williams, Joe
Williams, Janet
Williams, James
Williams, Vanessa
Williams, Camilla
Williams, Marion
Wilson, Olly Woodrow
Wilson, Nancy
Wilson, Mary
Winans, Vicki
Winans, BeBe
Winans Family
Winans, CeCe
Womack, Bobby
Wonder, Stevie
Zydeco, Buckwheat

Intimate Moments

Housing Authority of the City of Winston-Salem

HAWS

J. Reid Lawrence - *Executive Director*
A. Fulton Meachem, Jr. - *Deputy Executive Director*

Commissioners

William H. Andrews, *Chairman*
Ernest H. Pitt, *Vice Chairman*
Ms. Louise H. Davis
Bryan Rainbow
Mrs. Barbara G. White

Dear Maya Angelou,

What a distinct privilege and an honor it is for me to be afforded the opportunity of expressing sincere gratitude to God, for giving to all of us a "phenomenal woman of color." Reaching beyond racial, gender, religious and cultural boundaries, you have given us so much courage and hope. I, too, want to add myself to the countless millions of persons who are congratulating you on your outstanding accomplishments and acts of love.

Your influence on African American men is particularly noteworthy. Dr. Angelou, you impacted my life, as an African American man, at the grassroots stages. Perhaps, that's why it was so befitting and proper that you be asked to address one million African American men at the Million Man March in Washington, D.C. Many African American men depend on strong female role models to undergird their dreams and aspirations. We've needed the "gifts" of that special someone and you have not been a disappointment. For me, it has meant being honored by the prestigious Phi Beta Fraternity, as the 1999 Better Business Man of the Year . . . a dream and an aspiration. Thank you.

For the compassion and impact you have on American people, especially the less fortunate, we salute you. It truly goes beyond words. Your exemplary personification of the role as an "ambassador of good will" has increasingly opened the windows to the soul of people, young and old, rich and poor, black and white, and all social levels, to succeed and to "risk losing their ignorance." For this, we are eternally grateful.

The Housing Authority of the City of Winston-Salem is in the position of helping the less fortunate improve their way of living, strive for excellence in every area of their lives, and to never give up hope. Your impact, as a leader and an example, has enabled me, as Executive Director, to help them better themselves. I will continue your legacy through proactive programs and outreaches so that we, one person at a time, can make this world a better place in which to live.

Dr. Maya Angelou, you have made a mark that can never be erased. You have touched our hearts with the true essence of life, by bringing forth an understanding of ourselves whether in similarities or differences. As a result, we can now embrace each other with pureness of heart. We take this opportunity to thank you, again, for touching our hearts with your literary works and humanitarian efforts. On behalf of all Americans and myself, we salute you with God's love, blessings and peace.

Sincerely,

J. Reid Lawrence
Executive Director

JRL:avd

901 Cleveland Ave. ~ Winston-Salem, NC 27101 ~ Phone (336) 727-8500 ~ Fax (336) 777-8508

America Speaks . . .

Dear Dr. Angelou:

    Greetings! Just a few lines to say thanks for being a strong and gifted voice within America. You have touched my very essence.

    Just like you, my role has been to serve as a mentor to other young women. In February 1998, I had a chance to recite one of your literary masterpieces, *And Still I Rise*.

    Remember the television commercial that said "When E.F. Hutton speaks, people listen." Well, when Dr. Angelou speaks, people listen. My voice may not be as rich, deep and cultivated as yours. However, I enjoyed the opportunity to "play Dr. Maya Angelou," in a portrayal of the black woman during Black History month.

    Thank you for your contribution as a woman and a gifted human being. Life has been good to you and you have been good to us.

DARLENE YOUNG

★ ★ ★ ★ ★ ★ ★

Dear Dr. Maya Angelou:

    I am thankful for a vehicle, such as this one, to express my gratitude towards you and your contributions in my life. I discovered you in 1976, at the age of nine, while growing up in rural South Carolina.

    Though you were here long before my true awareness of you, my love for books led me to you. Your love for words and patterns of expressions have led me to a glorious life. Specifically, your works have given me a clear vision that might have otherwise been blurred by my circumstances and surroundings.

    Dr. Angelou, you have laid the foundation for women, like me, to aspire and to achieve. Your philosophies for living and the attainments of success have proven to be correct. Many aspects of those ingredients have been implemented and have given me my passport to a better understanding of our world.

    I have watched and observed you for more than two decades. I have taken heed to your advice because you have been a powerful source of inspiration. Seeds for my journey have been planted with care and the harvest has not been one of disappointment.

    In each area of my life, I have been blessed by our God. As a mother, wife, counselor, small business owner, and spiritual being, inner strength and motivation were gained from the examples that you set. You once told me that "any one person standing beside God constitutes the majority." I believe and I AM rewarded!

    Again, I am thankful to you and for you. As a direct result of your training, words of guidance, and influence, I am now uniquely positioned to also move mountains.

SANDRA D. BARNES

★ ★ ★ ★ ★ ★ ★

Georgia Black Chamber of Commerce

Affirmative Business Is Good Business

2577 Park Central Boulevard ~ Decatur, Georgia 30035 ~
Phone: 770-322-8980 ~ Fax: 770-322-0283
e-mail: gbcc@bellsouth.net   website: www.accessatlanta.com/community/groups/gbcc

---

Dear Maya Angelou:

It is truly an honor and a privilege for me to have this opportunity to express my sincere appreciation for all the things you have accomplished thus far. Your words have touched countless lives and shaped the destinies of so many people, both young and old.

We have been blessed to have a talented and dedicated person, like you, who have worked to make this a better place in which to live. With your many literary accomplishments, you have served as a role model and an inspiration to many aspiring artists. Your influence on people -- young, old, black and white -- has been and continues to be quite profound. Your words ring across cultural, racial, and gender lines, bringing the feeling of what we as "humans" feel. You have put them into words that are so simply and eloquently spoken.

And Still I Rise continues, for me, to be a soul-stirring piece that can apply to any situation where one finds oneself having to overcome adversity. Therefore, it is with a great deal of pleasure that I congratulate you on acquiring one of the most vital and pivotal roles to date -- that of addressing one million African-American men at the Million Man March in Washington, D.C. Our strong black women have always provided guidance and support for black men. I feel confident that you will continue to *Rise* to the occasion and provide your usual standard of excellence.

You have been such an inspiration to many. Your words have touched all our hearts and I thank you for all you have done and all you will continue to do.

...*and still I rise*...

Lou Walker
President

MIDDLE EAST CHILDREN'S ALLIANCE

On behalf of the 5,000 members of the Middle East Children's Alliance, I want to salute Dr. Maya Angelou. Dr. Angelou, we salute you for your unswerving devotion to human rights, your unwavering dedication to improving the lives of children worldwide, and your unstinting sharing of your enormous gifts on behalf of organizations and individuals in need. Her grace, dignity, and talent, have shamed all those who would deny anyone a chance for a full life based on color, race, sex or disability.

For all of our eleven years, Dr. Angelou has been a member of our advisory board. She demonstrated her typically great courage by joining an organization that supported Palestinian children at a time when that position was not popular in this country. Her public association with the Middle East Children's Alliance encouraged many thousands of other people to join us as well. Multiply our experience by the millions of others she has touched and you begin to understand the impact of Dr. Maya Angelou.

Barbara Lubin
Executive Director

905 Parker St. Berkeley, CA 94710   510/548-0542   fax:510/548-0543

Part Three
The Other Side of Greatness

I acknowledge immense debt to the griots [tribal poets] of Africa — where today it is rightly said that when a griot dies, it is as if a library has burned to the ground.

ALEX HALEY

Let a man in a garnet but burn with enough tensity and he will set fire to the whole world.

ANTOINE de SAINT EXUPERY

> He who controls the past commands the future.
> He who commands the future
> conquers the past.
>
> GEORGE ORWELL

the private side

APPOINTMENTS
- The University of Kansas appointed Angelou as a Writer-in-Residence in 1970.
- President Jimmy Carter appointed Angelou to the National Commission on the Observance of International Women's Year.
- President Gerald Ford appointed Angelou to the American Revolution Bicentennial Advisory Council.
- Angelou served as a lecturer at the University of California at Los Angeles in 1966.
- Angelou taught at the University of California in 1966 and the University of Kansas in 1970.
- Angelou served as Distinguished Visiting Professor to Wake-Forest University in 1974.
- Wichita State University appointed Angelou as Distinguished Visiting Professor in 1974.
- Angelou was appointed Distinguished Visiting Professor at California State University at Sacramento in 1974.
- Wake Forest University gave Angelou a lifetime appointment as Reynolds Professor of American Studies in 1981.
- In 1984, Angelou was named by Governor James Hunt to the Board of the North Carolina Arts Council.
- In 1996, Angelou was appointed as National Ambassador for the U.S. Committee for UNICEF.
- The Student Union Board of Governors appointed Angelou to the Lecture Committee for large and small lectures.

AWARDS/HONORS
- The Ladies Home Journal named Angelou "Woman of the Year in Communications" in 1976.
- In 1975, The Ladies Home Journal gave Angelou the "Woman of the Year in Communications" award.
- Angelou is the recipient of the 1983 Matrix Award.
- In 1987, Angelou received the North Carolina Award in Literature.
- The Ladies Home Journal voted Angelou "Top 100 Most Influential Women" in 1983.
- Angelou received the Horatio Alger Award in 1992.
- Essence Magazine named Angelou "Woman of the Year" in 1992.
- Angelou was named "Distinguished Woman of North Carolina" in 1992.
- On May 17, 1992, Angelou was given a bronze star at 6337 Delmar Street on the St. Louis Walk of Fame. She received the star in the Field of Achievement for Literature. Eugene B. Redmond, Poet Laureate of East St. Louis accepted the award for Ms. Angelou. Angelou joined other celebrities such as Josephine Baker, Chuck Berry, Scott Joplin, Lou Brock and Miles Davis.
- On July 11, 1998, Angelou was inducted into the National Women's Hall of Fame in Seneca Falls, New York. Angelou was awarded the "Order of Kilimanjaro Award." The "Order of Kilimanjaro Award" is the highest honor to be bestowed on anyone by indigenous Africans to someone living in the U.S.
- Angelou was one of the 12 Black American writers honored by Ghana and Uganda with a postage stamp in their name. Annually, the NAACP gives the "NAACP Spingarn Award" to a person of African descent, who has the highest achievement in a field of endeavor for a preceding year or years. Angelou was the recipient of that award.
- The University of Hawaii's Board of Regents presented Angelou with the first-ever Medal of Distinction.

BOARDS
- The American Film Institute appointed Angelou to the Board of Trustees. She has served in that position since 1975.

DEGREES
- Angelou has received over 50 honorary doctorate degrees from several universities. Some of those universities include Smith College (1975), Mills College (1975) and Lawrence University (1976).

FAMILY
- On February 2, 1976, Maya Angelou became a grandmother with the birth of Colin Ashanti Johnson.
- Angelou becomes a great-grandmother when Caylin Nicole Johnson was born on February 1, 1998.
- Angelou's son, Guy Johnson, was hired by Western Airlines as their first African-American executive.
- In December 1998, Angelou's son becomes a published author with his first novel *Standing at the Scratch Line*. Random House published Johnson's novel.

FELLOWSHIPS
- In 1970, Angelou became the recipient of the Yale University Fellowship.
- In 1975, Angelou was the recipient of the Rockefeller Foundation Scholar in Italy.

MEMBERSHIPS
- Angelou is an Alpha Kappa Alpha Sorority member. Angelou is a member of the Directors Guild, Equity and the Harlem Writers Guild.
- Angelou is also a member of the American Federation of Television and Radio Artists.
- Angelou serves as a member of the Advisory Board for the Women's Prison Association.

PUBLICATIONS
Listed below are articles and interviews in various U.S. periodicals about Dr. Maya Angelou

- *Architectural Digest,* May 1994, p. 32
- *Black Stars*, September 1979, p. 46
- *Black World*, July 1975
- *Black World*, August 1974, pp. 10-18
- *Black American Literature Forum*, Summer 1990, pp. 221-35, 257-76
- *Black Scholar*, January-February 1977, pp. 44-53; Summer 1982
- *Booklist*, September 1, 1993, p.2
- *Brown Sugar*, Donald Bogle, p. 182

- *Chicago Tribune Bookworld*, March 23, 1986
- *Chicago Tribune*, July 15, 1979, sec. 12, p. 3
- *Chicago Tribune*, November 1, 1981
- *Christian Century*, November 23, 1988, pp. 1031-2
- *CLA Journal*, Dec., 1976, pp. 273-291
- *College Literature*, October 1991, pp. 64-79
- *Current Biography*, 1974, pp. 12-15
- *Current Biography*, February 1994, p. 7
- *Detroit Free Press*, May 9, 1986
- *Ebony Success Library*, v.1, p.13
- *Ebony*, April 1970, pp. 62-70
- *Ebony*, August 1978, p. 160
- *Encore*, September 12, 1977, pp. 28-32
- *Encore*, Spring, 1972, p. 61
- *Entertainment Weekly*, October 21, 1994, p. 83
- *Essence*, August 1975, p. 42
- *Essence*, May 1983, pp. 112-114
- *Essence*, January 1980, pp. 14
- *Essence*, May 1972, p. 76
- *Harper's*, November 1972
- *Harper's*, March 1994, p. 28
- *Harvard Educational Review*, November 1970
- *Index to Black American Writers*, Dorothy W. Campbell, p. 49
- *Jet*, October 21, 1971, p. 45
- *Jet*, August 26, 1971, p. 57
- *Ladies Home Journal*, May 1976, p. 75
- *Library Journal*, November 1, 1995, p. 82
- *Library Journal*, November 1, 1994, p. 88
- *Library Journal*, October 1, 1995, p. 102
- *Life*, Dec. 31, 1971, p. 54
- *Living Black American Authors*, Ann Shockley, pp. 4-5
- *Los Angeles Times Book Review*, April 13, 1986
- *Los Angeles Times Book Review*, August 9, 1987
- *Los Angeles Times Book Review*, October 3, 1993
- *Los Angeles Times*, May 29, 1983
- *Ms.*, January 1977

- *National Review*, November 29, 1993, p. 76
- *Negro History Bulletin*, May/June, 1977, pp. 694-695
- *New York Times*, April 22, 1979, p. D-35
- *New York Times*, December 5, 1992, p. L8
- *New York Times Book Review*, December 19, 1993, p. 18
- *New Republic*, July 6, 1974
- *New Republic*, October 3, 1994, p. 10
- *New York Times Book Review*, June 16, 1974
- *New York Times*, February 25, 1970
- *Newsweek*, March 2, 1970
- *Observer* (London), April 1, 1984; November 28, 1993; Dec. 17, 1995
- *People*, August 25, 1975; pp. 56-59
- *People*, November 27, 1978, p. 96
- *People*, March 8, 1982, pp. 92-99
- *People*, December 5, 1977, p. 113
- *Publishers Weekly*, September 12, 1994, p. 91
- *Publishers Weekly*, September 20, 1993, p. 71
- *San Francisco Examiner* Datebook, June 16, 1974, p. 7
- *School Library Journal*, October 1994, p. 107
- *School Library Journal*, May 1994, p. 144
- *School Library Journal*, March 1994, p. 224
- *Southern Living*, January 1994, p. 66
- *Third Woman*, Dexter Fisher, p. 287
- *Time*, March 31, 1986
- *Times* (London), September 29, 1986
- *Times Literary Supplement*, February 17, 1974
- *Times Literary Supplement*, June 14, 1985
- *Times Literary Supplement*, January 24, 1986
- *Tribune Books*, September 11, 1994, p. 8
- *Urban West*, June 1970, p. 29
- *Village Voice*, July 11, 1974
- *Village Voice*, October 28, 1981
- *Washington Post Bookworld*, May 11, 1986
- *Washington Post Bookworld*, June 26, 1983
- *Washington Post Bookworld*, October 4, 1981
- *Washington Post*, October 13, 1981

- *Washington Post Bookworld*, September 15, 1993, p. 4
- *Washington Post Bookworld*, December 5, 1993, p. 25
- *World Literature Today*, August 1995, p. 800

TID BITS

- Angelou drove racing cars in Mexico before she turned 20. Angelou is one of the few African-American authors to have three books placed on the New York Times Best Seller for 10 consecutive weeks.
- Growing up in the home of a spiritual grandmother, Angelou became acquainted with the church. She attributes the language of the church as part being an intricate part of her writing today.
- Many schools and libraries bear the name of Dr. Maya Angelou.
- Angelou's resume is more than five pages in length.
- It is reported that Angelou earns approximately $15,000 per lecture.
- Angelou speaks many languages fluently, such as West African Fanti, Italian, Arabic, Spanish and French.
- Many have claimed Angelou to be one of the best cooks in the world. Often, she has her friends over to her home for delicious meals and fellowship. Angelou has said, "My dear, my greens spread like butter."
- For those other than her friends or acquaintances, she likes to be called "Ms. or Dr. Angelou."
- To begin writing, Angelou goes to a rented hotel room near her home in North Carolina. Her writing supplies include a Roget's Thesaurus, a dictionary, the Holy Bible, a yellow pad and a deck of cards for solitaire.
- Angelou has been a contributor of articles, short stories, and poems to such periodicals such as Harper's, Ebony, Ghanian Times, Mademoiselle, Redbook and the Black Scholar.

Part Four

Appendix

Acknowledgements

All thanks, praises, glory and honor goes to my Lord and Saviour, Jesus Christ. Thank God that through Jesus Christ, I am more than a conqueror. Without Him, I am nothing, but with Him, I am somebody and can do all things, including the impossible.

To my father, Rev. Frederick Douglass Hobbs (1926-1987) whose apostolic and prophetic mantel I proudly wear. Thanks Daddy for teaching me the rudiments of life; trust and serve God with all your heart, mind, body and soul. I love you.

To my mother, Viola Marie Hobbs, who taught me how to love and to be the essence and epitome of the word "woman." Mom, you're absolutely fabulous and I love you.

To my sister, Iris Lynette Hobbs-Dixon and my brothers, Frederick Dewitt Hobbs and Harold Joseph Hobbs — we're destined to leave a mark on this world that can never be erased. God bless you richly in all that you undertake for the Kingdom of God.

To all my aunts, uncles, and cousins, on my mother and father's side of the family (Hobbs, Reed, Freeman, Brock, Patton, Patterson, Shepherd, Walker, Yelder), in-laws, nieces and nephews — keep striving for excellence in everything you do. To my real friends, you know who you are . . . I love you.

Heartfelt thanks are in order for Towanda Spencer (the "True Friend") who has been my special gift of love and support – my heart's love for you; Ellen Sanders (the "Ms. Hollywood") for sharing, caring and supporting me at all the right times – much love always from the heart; Leon B. Howard (the "Portraiteer") who paints love on the canvas – a million thank yous; a lifetime of thanks to Marcella Drula at Spectrum Publishing in Fairfax, Virginia, for always coming through for me with the best artwork for book covers this side of heaven; Kathleen Myers (the "Artist") for being one of the greatest design artists on the face of this earth, a million thanks; and, Donna Teel-Scruggs who, to me, is a wonderful and skilled editor and proofreader – all my love.

Bibliography

Introduction
1. Richard Bach, *Jonathan Livingston Seagull* (New York: Macmillan, 1970).

Part 1 - The Incomparable Dr. Maya Angelou
2. James Baldwin, *I Know Why the Caged Bird Sings* (New York: Random House, 1969).
3. William Shakespeare, *As You Like It* (New Cambridge Shakespeare), Act 2, Scene 7, Jamieson (Editor) (Massachusetts: Cambridge University Press, 2000)

Humble Beginnings
4. Patricia Holt, *San Francisco Chronicle Book Review*, April 12, 1998.

Becoming a Legend
5. *Writers Digest*, 1975.

Reflections on Life
6. Lisa Funderberg, *Power Moves (A Conversation with Maya Angelou and Eleanor Holmes Norton)* (Illinois: Essence Communications, 1998).
7. Ibid.
8. David Frost, *An Interview with Maya Angelou by David Frost*, reprinted with permission from WNET/Channel 13 in *The New Sun Newspaper*, Dunton Corporation, 1997.
9. Dave Iverson, *An Interview with Dr. Maya Angelou: State of the Union*, 1993.
10. Ibid.
11. Ibid.
12. Ibid.
13. Ibid.
14. HomeArts: *Maya Angelou — A Western Canon Jr.* (The Hearst Corporation, 1997).

Part 2 - Dr. Maya Angelou's Lifetime Contributions
15. Toni Morrison, *Nobel Lectures, Literature 1991-1995* (Singapore: World Scientific Publishing Company, 1999).
16. Emily Dickinson, *Poems by Emily Dickinson*, Second Series, edited by two of her friends, Mabel Loomis Todd and T.W. Higginson (Massachusetts: Roberts Brothers, 1896).

Part 3 - The Other Side of Greatness
17. Alex Haley, *We Must Honor Our Ancestors*, Ebony Magazine, August 1986.
18. Antoine de Saint Exupery, *Wind, Sand, and Stars* (Unknown: 1939).

Photo Credits

Photo credits are listed by page number and source as follows:

Page 24, Library of Congress, Prints and Photographs Division, Carl VanVechten Collection; 37, Library of Congress, Prints and Photographs Division, Carl VanVechten Collection; 52, AP/Wide World Photos, Inc., Library of Congress, Prints and Photographs Division, Carl VanVechten Collection; 84, Schomberg Center for Research in Black Culture, NY; 95, Courtesy of the Maya Angelou Elementary School, Miami, FL; 124, AP/Wide World Photos and Courtesy of the Library of Congress; 136-137, Archive Photos, NY; 155, Library of Congress, Prints and Photographs Division, Carl VanVechten Collection.

Index

A

A Brave and Startling Truth (Angelou), 122
Adjoa Amissah, 41, 130
African Review, 40
Ailey, Alvin, 40
Ajax, 130
Al and Rita Show, 40
Ali, Muhammad, 164
All Day Long, 127
Allen, Debbie, 42
Alley Theater, 131
Alpha Kappa Alpha Sorority, 185
The American Film Institute, 184
And Still I Rise (Angelou), 67, 122, 125, 130, 175
Angelos, Tosh, 40
Angelou on Burns (Angelou), 129
Angelou, Maya, 3, 5, 11, 13-16, 21, 25, 30, 39, 43, 48, 54, 58, 94, 98, 105, 111, 112, 115, 116, 118-122, 124-127, 132-134, 142, 145, 148, 149, 156, 159, 160, 162-164, 166, 175, 185, 188
Annie Clark Tanner Lecture, 149
Arab Observer, 40
Asante of Ghana, 130
Associated Press, 162
Atlantic Records, 131
Ayer, Ethel, 40

B

Baker, Josephine, 184
Baldwin, James, 23, 40, 57
Bancroft, Anne, 121
Basquiat, Jean Michel, 121
The Beacon Book of Essays (Martin), 125
Bearing Witness (Angelou), 114
Been Found (Ashford and Simpson), 126
Belafonte, Harry, 160
Benedict, Dirk, 120
Berry, Chuck, 184
Bethune, Mary McLeod, 43
Bjorkman, Stig, 120
Black African Heritage Series, 129
The Black Family Pledge (Angelou), 125, 156
Black Film Center/Archive, 159
Black Pearls: The Poetry of Maya Angelou (Angelou), 118
Black! Blues! Black!, 57, 130
The Blacks, 40, 131
Blue Angel, 39
Blues Traveler, 131

Body and Soul Conference, 145
Bogle, Donald, 160, 185
Bolin, Jane M., 167
Bond, Julian, 129
Boto, Nyo, 129
Bouchet, Edward, 94
Bowser, Pearl, 160
Boyers, Sara, 121
Bradley, Ed, 134
Brewster Place, 58
Brock, Lou, 184
Bronze star, 184
Brooks, Gwendolyn, 116, 125, 134
The Brothers Karamzov (Dostoyevsky), 92
Brown, Alma, 163
Brown, Les, 145
Brown, Ronald, 165
Burnett, Charles, 160
Burns, Robert, 95, 129
Burstyn, Ellen, 121, 131

C

Cabaret for Freedom, 40, 130
California State University, 183
California Labor School, 27
Calypso Heatwave, 40, 131
Cambridge, Godfrey, 114
Caribbean and African Cooking (Angelou and Grant), 118
Carter, President Jimmy, 165, 183
Casey, Bernie, 160
Center Theater Group, 131
Charles Stewart Mott Foundation, 160
Cher, 123
Child Protection Team and Family Centre, 163
The Civil War (A Diary), 131
The Clawing Within, 41, 132
Clinton, President William Jefferson, 124, 148
Cole, Natalie, 130
Collins, Marva, 96
The Collected Poems (Dunbar), 93
The Complete Collected Poems of Maya Angelou (Angelou), 125
Cortez, Carol, 160
Cosby, Bill, 160
Cosmopolitan Magazine, 58

D

Dahomey, 130

Dan dancers, 130
Davis, Ossie, 129, 162
Davis, Miles, 184
Dee, Ruby, 170
Delessert, Etienne, 119
The Denver Post, 115
Diaz, Maria B., 160
Dickens, Charles, 92
Dickinson, Emily, 109
Didion, Joan, 125
Dillard, Annie 125
Dion, Celine, 123
Directors Guild, 185
Distinguished Visiting Professor, 183
Douglas, Frederick, 117
Down in the Delta, 58, 120
Dunbar, Paul Laurence, 93

E
Eliot, T.S., 161
Encounters, 131
Ensemble Theatre, 130
Equity, 185
Essence Magazine, 184
Eugene Agnes Meyer Foundation, 163
Even the Stars Look Lonesome (Angelou), 118, 119

F
Families Alive Conference, 149
Feelings, Tom, 122, 124
Feiffer, Jules, 57
Feu, Paul Du, 58
Field of Achievement for Literature, 184
Flowers, Bertha, 113
Ford Foundation, 160
Ford, President Gerald, 183
Forman, James, Jr., 163
Fox, Matthew, 145
Freeman, Mr., 26
Freeman, Morgan, 127
Frost, Robert, 148

G
Gather Together in My Name (Angelou), 112
Gentry, Minnie, 120
George Washington University, 163
Georgia, Georgia, 30, 58, 120
Getting Up Stayed on My Mind, 131

Ghanian Times, 40
Ghanian Broadcasting Corporation, 40
Gillespie, Bob, 129
Ginsberg, Allen, 164
Giovanni, Nikki, 123
Glover, Danny, 131
Go Tell It on the Mountain (Baldwin), 92
Golden Eagle Award, 127
Gossett, Louis, Jr., 40
Gowain, Shakfi, 145
Graham, Martha, 40
Grant, Rosamund, 118
Gray, Marian, 116
Greeting the Morning (Angelou), 111, 119
GWP Records, 58

H
Hakima Theatre, 40
Haley, Alex, 134, 181
Hampton University, 160
Harlem Literary Guild, 40
Havens, Richie, 164
The Heart of a Woman (Angelou), 49, 114, 132, 133
Henderson, Annie, 25
Hicks, Dr. H. Beecher, Jr., 11, 14, 116
Holiday, Billie, 39
Holt, Patricia, 26
Hope, Bob, 159
Horatio Alger Award, 184
Horne, Lena, 117
Hounsou, Djimon, 127
Housing Our Families, 162
How to Make an American Quilt, 58, 116, 121
Huggins, Nathan I., 111
Hughes, Langston, 116, 117, 122
Hunt, Governor James, 183
Hurston, Zora Neale, 117

I
I Shall Not Be Moved (Angelou), 124, 133
I Know Why the Caged Bird Sings (Angelou), 13, 36, 49, 54, 57, 113, 127, 129, 133, 156
I Have a Dream (Kallen), 45, 119
The Inheritors, 129

J
Jackson Hole Wildlife Film Festival, 129
Johnson, Bailey, 25

Johnson, Colin Ashanti, 185
Johnson, Guy, 27, 126, 159, 185
Johnson, James Weldon, 116, 148
Johnson, Marguerite, 25, 39, 113, 119
Johnson, Vivian Baxter, 25, 26
Jones, James Earl, 40, 111, 114
Jones, Quincy, 128, 160
Joplin, Scott, 184
Jordan, Barbara, 57
Jordan, June, 164
Journey of the Heart (Pettit), 119

K
Kelly, Sharon Pratt, 167
Kennedy, Ellen C., 116
Kennedy, President John, 148
King, Coretta Scott, 57, 111, 120
King, Rev. Dr. Martin Luther, Jr., 45, 114, 148
King, Sarah E., 111, 119
Knight, Gladys, 32
Kofi and His Magic (Angelou), 121

L
Ladies Home Journal, 184, 186
Lafayette Country Training School, 26
Lear, Norman, 59
The Least of These, 41, 132
Lee, Spike, 121, 125
The Legacy, 129
Liberty Records, 126
Lincoln, Mary Todd, 131
The Little Prince (Saint-Exupery), 92
The Living Edens, 130
Look Away, 131
Los Angeles Times, 115, 186

M
Make, Vusumzi, 40, 114
Mandella, Nelson, 96
Mark Taper Forum, 130, 131
Martin, Wendy, 125
Matrix Award, 184
Maya Angelou Community Initiative Project, 162
Maya Angelou Elementary School, 160
The Maya Angelou Poetry Collection (Angelou), 126
Maya Angelou Project, 162
McCarthy, Linda, 164
McCarthy, Paul, 164
McConaughey, Matthew, 127
McDaniel, Hattie, 60
McKenna, Terence, 145
Mead, Margaret, 125
Medal of Distinction, 184

Medca, 40
The Miami Herald, 115
Michigan State University, 148
Million Man March, 148
Million Woman March, 148
Mills College, 185
Mirikitani, Janice, 126, 159
Miss Calypso, 40, 126
Mission High School, 27
Mobil Oil, 163
Moon on a Rainbow Shawl, 131
Moore, Mary Tyler, 42
Morris Gwendolyn Cafritz Foundation, 163
Morrison, Toni, 109
Mother Courage, 41
Mother Teresa, 164
Mt. Zion Baptist Church, 162
My Painted House, My Friendly Chicken and Me (Angelou and Courtney), 122

N
NAACP, 184
National Book Award, 57
National Council of Churches of Christ, 162
National Education Television, 57
National Society for the Prevention of Cruelty to Children, 163
The Negritude Poets (Angelou and Kennedy), 116
New York Times Book Review, 115, 187
Nixon, Dr. Lois LaCivita, 116
North Carolina Arts Council, 183
Not Without Laughter (Angelou and Hughes), 116
Now Sheba Sings the Song (Angelou and Feelings), 124

O
Oasis Recording, 129, 130
Obie award, 40, 131
Octavio Viciedo, 160
Oh Pray My Wings Are Gonna Fit Me Well (Angelou), 124
On the Pulse of Morning (Angelou), 124, 126, 148
Orwell, George, 183

P
Page, Geraldine, 131
Parks, Gordon, 129
Payton, John, 163
Peale, Norman Vincent, 28
Pettit, Jayne, 119
Phenomenal Woman (Angelou), 13, 91, 125, 133, 142
Poe, Edgar Allan, 151

192

Poetic Justice, 121, 125
Poitier, Sidney, 160
Popper, John, 131
Porgy and Bess, 39, 113
Powell, General Colin, 58, 161
Price, Florence B., 134
Primus, Pearl, 39
Project Open Hand, 159
Public Welfare Foundation, 163
Purple Onion, 39

R
Raleigh Memorial Auditorium, 149
Redfield, James, 145
Reynolds Professor, 183
Right to Rock Network, 166
Ringgold, Faith, 114
Roots, 120, 129, 134
Ross, Diana, 128
Rustin, Bayard, 40
Ryder, Winona, 121

S
Sanders, Bernie, 164
Sands, Diana, 120
Schwarzenegger, Arnold, 164
See Forever, 163
Shakespeare, William, 23
Shapiro, Miles, 111, 120
Shaw, George Bernard, 57
Shaw University, 149
Sheen, Martin, 164
Shuker, Nancy, 120
Silvera, Frank, 40
Simmons, Jean, 121
Simpson, Lorna, 114
Singleton, John, 121, 125
Sister, Sister, 58, 129
The Slave Coast, 130
Smith, Lois, 121
Snipes, Wesley, 120
Soros Foundation, 163
Soul Looks Back in Wonder (Angelou), 122
Southern Christian Leadership Conference, 40, 114, 130
Spain, Valerie, 112, 120
Spielberg, Steven, 127, 139
St. Louis Walk of Fame, 184
Stamps, 14, 25, 119
Standing at the Scratch Line (Johnson), 185
Strauss, Robert, 163
Streetcar conductor, 27, 43
Sweet Briar College, 149

T
There is a Moral to It All, 164
Thuna, Leona, 129
Todd, Susan, 129
Touched By An Angel, 130
Toure, Askia, 122
Trials, Tribulations, and Celebrations: African-American Perspectives on Health, Illness, Aging, and Loss (Gray), 116
Turner, Tina, 128
Twain, Mark, 39
Twentieth Century Fox Television, 41
Tyson, Cicely, 40

U
UNICEF, 183
United Nations, 122, 145
University of Ghana, 40
University of Kansas, 57, 183

V
Village Gate, 131
The Voyage of the Amistad, 127

W
Wake Forest University, 183
Walker, Alice, 116
Walters, Barbara, 57
Washington, Booker T., 71
The Washington Post Book World, 115
Weber State University, 149
Western Airlines, 185
Whitaker, Forest, 59
Whitman, Walt, 123
Wichita State University, 183
Wilder, L. Douglas, 167
Williams, Vanessa, 123
Wilson, Frederica, 160
Winfrey, Oprah, 58
Wonder, Stevie, 98, 123
Woodard, Alfre, 120
Woolsley, Ralph B., 129
Worldfest 1996, 150

X
X, Malcolm, 45, 114

Y
Yale University fellow, 57
Yoruba, 130
Young, Andrew Jr., 129, 167

About the Author

Dr. Avaneda Dorenza Hobbs has studied and been involved with some of the premiere colleges in the United States. A recipient of a bachelor's degree in Sociology/Anthropology, Avaneda graduated from Virginia Wesleyan College, one of America's top 100 colleges. She then furthered her education by receiving master and doctorate degrees in educational administration.

Having grown up in the church all of her life, Avaneda spent countless hours with her father learning how to build and to grow religious institutions. Prior to his death in 1987, Avaneda helped to establish and build the Sword of the Spirit Ministries church left here by her father, Reverend Frederick D. Hobbs. Today, Dr. Hobbs works closely with organizations to help with church administration, church growth, marketing and advertising and developing religious educational institutions. Dr. Hobbs also worked very closely with the late Archbishop Dr. Benson A. Idahosa and was responsible for laying the framework for Christian Faith University, a fully accredited bible college in Nigeria, West Africa.

Dr. Avaneda Hobbs has served as Vice President of Marketing and Product Development for TRD, Inc. She joined TRD after a two-year tenure as the Executive Director of Institutional Development for the World Resource Outreach Company. Before the above positions, Dr. Hobbs served as the National Public Relations Director for GGE, Inc. In that position, she helped to secure such notable personalities as FCC Commissioner James Quello, to garner support for minority entrepreneurs engaged in purchasing broadcasting stations.

Dr. Hobbs has performed in concerts with Grammy award winning artists such as James Cleveland, Daryl Coley, Sissy Houston, Richard Smallwood, the Winans, Beau Williams, Walter Hawkins, DeLeon Richards, Edwin Hawkins, Myrna Summers, and the Governing Board of Bishops for the Church of God In Christ, to name a few.

A highlight in Avaneda Hobbs' career, as a vocalist, was her appearance as the guest soloist for the 1995 Martin Luther King National Prayer Breakfast in Columbus, Ohio. The prayer breakfast was televised "live," with over 6,000 people in attendance. The breakfast was attended by the Governor of Ohio, the Mayor of Columbus, Ohio, the late Olympic Gold Medalist Florence Joyner Griffith, and other dignitaries from the educational, financial, social and political arenas. Further, Dr. Hobbs was the guest soloist for a recording with Morehouse College's Martin Luther King International Chapel Choir, Spellman College and Emory University.

Avaneda Hobbs holds membership on several corporation boards. The most notable are the Jerusalem 2000 Millennium Council and The Smithsonian Institution's African-American Museum. Dr. Hobbs also holds memberships in the National Association of Female Executives and the National Black Religious Broadcasters.

Dr. Hobbs is listed in Marquis 51st Edition of *Who's Who In America*, Marquis 25th Edition of *Who's Who In The East*, Marquis 19th Edition of *Who's Who Of American Women*, and the International Biographical Centre's 13th Edition of *The World Who's Who of Women*. She is also the recipient of a Washington, D.C. Mayoral Commendation for Active and Cooperative Leadership award. Dr. Hobbs was selected in 1992 to participate in a Congressional and White House briefing on the African-American Family with President George Bush and Chief Justice Clarence Thomas.

Avaneda Hobbs is the 1997 recipient of the prestigious Telly award. Dr. Hobbs won the award, out of 9,000 entries, for her contributions as a writer and researcher for the videotape series titled *Community Economic Development: Challenges and Opportunities of Communities in Transition*. In November 1997, Dr. Hobbs was selected to open the African-American Cultural Expo as a lecturer on African-American religious history, with such notable personalities as Charlie Sifford, the first black PGA golfer and the renowned Dick Gregory.

Featured in the 2000 release of the *Women of Color Holy Bible* are three articles written by Dr. Avaneda Hobbs. Dr. Hobbs is also a frequent author at the Walt Disney World Company in Orlando, Florida.

CAP Publishing's Best Selling Publications

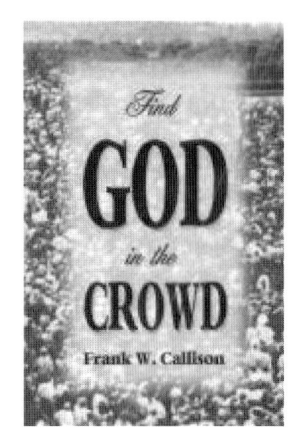

Find God in the Crowd by Frank C. Callison
Find God in the Crowd is an exciting and intriguing tale. The setting is a rural suburb of Denver, Colorado, and the characters are everyday folk. The intrigue and excitement come from an old chest given to the main character and startling events in the characters' lives. Intrigue erupts into a worldwide search for "the ideal citizen." The story examines the very topical concern of how we judge others. In the end, the reader is left to judge the main character — a shiftless roustabout, who, like a coin, proves to have two sides.
ISBN: 1-878898-21-3; Novel; Paperback; 5-1/2x8-1/2; $15.95; 194 pages

From the Garden of Eden to America by Avaneda D. Hobbs, Ed.D.
From the Garden of Eden discusses the biblical beginnings of the black man's slavery, the scriptural significance of the Garden of Eden and the history of the races, the origin of the American black church, and a detailed description of all black religious bodies in the U.S. Original photos of the denomination's leaders, from the 1700's to the 1900's, are included. Further, it examines the ingredients required for training effective black leaders in building churches and their role in building an influential church, from an evangelistic point of view.
ISBN: 1-878898-04-3; Black History/Religion; Paperback; 6x9; $19.95; 248 pages

Sonnets from the Soul by Tracy L. Wells
Poet Wells has written a beautiful and inspiring collection of poetry. Covering every imaginable topical area faced by mankind, Wells brilliantly captures the life and lifestyles of mankind only the way a "pen" can.
ISBN: 1-878898-25-6; Poetry; Paperback; 5-1/2x8-1/2; $12.00; 104 pages

Order Form

Type your name, shipping address and telephone number:

Name _____

Company Name _____

Shipping Address _____

City _____

State/Province _____ ZIP/Postal Code _____

Daytime Phone (_____) _____
(In case we have a question about your order)

Please check your product choice here:

DESCRIPTION	QUANTITY	PRICE	TOTAL

Calculate your total cost and indicate method of payment:

Product Cost	$	PAYMENT METHODS (Make checks payable CAP Publishing)
US Sales Tax	$	American Express
Freight	$	Mastercard
Total Cost	$	VISA
		Credit Card No.
		Expiration Date
		Cardholder's Signature

If ordering in large quantities, please call for special pricing

DIVERSE BOOKS
CAP Publishing & Literary Co., LLC
P.O. Box 471403
Forestville, Maryland 20747
www.cap-publishing.com
e-mail: drneda@pobox.com